Jeremy Keith

GOING OFFLINE

MORE FROM A BOOK APART

Conversational Design
Erika Hall

The New CSS Layout
Rachel Andrew

Accessibility for Everyone
Laura Kalbag

Practical Design Discovery
Dan Brown

Demystifying Public Speaking
Lara Hogan

JavaScript for Web Designers
Mat Marquis

Practical SVG
Chris Coyier

Design for Real Life
Eric Meyer & Sara Wachter-Boettcher

Git for Humans
David Demaree

Going Responsive
Karen McGrane

Visit abookapart.com for our full list of titles.

Publisher: Jeffrey Zeldman
Designer: Jason Santa Maria
Executive Director: Katel LeDû
Managing Editor: Lisa Maria Martin
Technical Editor: Amber Wilson and Jake Archibald
Copyeditor: Kate Towsey
Proofreader: Katel LeDû
Book Producer: Ron Bilodeau
Illustration Producer: Jon Long

ISBN: 978-1-937557-70-6

A Book Apart
New York, New York
http://abookapart.com

10 9 8 7 6 5 4 3 2 1

TABLE OF CONTENTS

FOREWORD

WE OFTEN TALK GLEEFULLY about the open and ubiquitous nature of the web, but it has an Achilles' heel: network connectivity. If your career is spent working on the web, chances are you might rarely encounter networking issues in your day-to-day life. When it comes to networks, many of us are spoiled with sweet, sweet speed and incredible reliability. We take it for granted that everyone in the world experiences the web like we do.

With an uncertain network connection, the web can be elusive. Broken page layouts. Missing functionality. Lost images. Dinosaurs. Broken hearts. Frustration.

With no network at all, the web ceases to exist.

Over the years, scores of people far smarter than I have looked for ways to help the web overcome its complete dependence on the network. Browser caching, Application Cache, Local (and Session) Storage, and client-side databases have all helped to some degree (well, maybe not AppCache) but these technologies have been somewhat limited in both scope and capability.

Then along came the service workers. Service workers are one of the most powerful tools we've had at our disposal, enabling us to control how we handle network requests. They even enable us to decide whether to make a network request at all. Of course, that power also gives us the ability to completely break our sites—if we're not careful.

Which brings me to the book you hold in your hands. In *Going Offline*, Jeremy Keith breaks down heady concepts into approachable prose and easy-to-follow code examples. He also points out service worker gotchas and shows you how to deftly avoid them. Invest a scant few hours with this book, and you'll gain a solid understanding of how to put this new technology to work for you right away. No, really—within fifteen to twenty minutes of putting it down.

Armed with the knowledge you gain from Jeremy's words, I have no doubt you'll do wonders to improve the resilience of the web.

—Aaron Gustafson

1
INTRODUCING SERVICE WORKERS

BUSINESSES ARE BUILT ON THE WEB. Without the web, Twitter couldn't exist. Facebook couldn't exist. And not just businesses—Wikipedia couldn't exist. Your favorite blog couldn't exist without the web. The web doesn't favor any one kind of use. It's been deliberately designed to accommodate many and varied activities.

Just as many wonderful things are built upon the web, the web itself is built upon the internet. Though we often use the terms *web* and *internet* interchangeably, the World Wide Web is just one application that uses the internet as its plumbing. Email, for instance, is another.

Like the web, the internet was designed to allow all kinds of services to be built on top of it. The internet is a network of networks, all of them agreeing to use the same protocols to shuttle packets of data around. Those packets are transmitted down fiber-optic cables across the ocean floor, bounced around with Wi-Fi or radio signals, or beamed from satellites in freakin' space.

As long as these networks are working, the web is working. But sometimes networks go bad. Mobile networks have a tendency to get flaky once you're on a train or in other situations where you're, y'know, mobile. Wi-Fi networks work fine until you try to use one in a hotel room (their natural enemy).

When the network fails, the web fails. That's just the way it is, and there's nothing we can do about it. Until now.

WEAVING THE WEB

For as long as I can remember, the World Wide Web has had an inferiority complex. Back in the '90s, it was outshone by CD-ROMs (ask your parents). They had video, audio, and a richness that the web couldn't match. But they lacked links—you couldn't link from something in one CD-ROM to something in another CD-ROM. They faded away. The web grew.

Later, the web technologies of HTML, CSS, and JavaScript were found wanting when compared to the whiz-bang beauty of Flash. Again, Flash movies were much richer than regular web pages. But they were also black boxes. The Flash format seemed superior to the open standards of the web, and yet the very openness of those standards made the web an unstoppable force. Flash—under the control of just one company—faded away. The web grew.

These days it's native apps that make the web look like an underachiever. Like Flash, they're under the control of individual companies instead of being a shared resource like the web. Like Flash, they demonstrate all sorts of capabilities that the web lacks, such as access to device APIs and, crucially, the ability to work even when there's no network connection.

The history of the web starts to sound like an endless retelling of the fable of the tortoise and the hare. CD-ROMs, Flash, and native apps outshine the web in the short term, but the web always seems to win the day somehow.

Each of those technologies proved very useful for the expansion of web standards. In a way, Flash was like the R&D department for HTML, CSS, and JavaScript. Smooth animations, embedded video, and other great features first saw the light of day in Flash. Having shown their usefulness, they later appeared in web standards. The same thing is happening with native apps. Access to device features like the camera and the accelerometer is beginning to show up in web browsers. Most exciting of all, we're finally getting the ability for a website to continue working even when the network isn't available.

SERVICE WORKERS

The technology that makes this bewitching offline sorcery possible is a browser feature called *service workers*. You might have heard of them. You might have heard that they're something to do with JavaScript, and technically they are...but conceptually they're very different from other kinds of scripts.

Usually when you're writing some JavaScript that's going to run in a web browser, it's all related to the document currently being displayed in the browser window. You might want to listen out for events triggered by the user interacting with the document (clicks, swipes, hovers, etc.). You might want to update the contents of the document: add some markup here, remove some text there, manipulate some values somewhere else. The sky's the limit. And it's all made possible thanks to the Document Object Model (DOM), a representation of what the browser is rendering. Through the combination of the DOM and JavaScript—DOM scripting, if you will—you can conjure up all sorts of wonderful magic.

Well, a service worker can't do any of that. It's still a script, and it's still written in the same language—JavaScript—but it has no access to the DOM. Without any DOM scripting capabilities, this kind of script might seem useless at first glance. But there's an advantage to having a script that never needs to interact with the current document. Adding, editing, and deleting parts of the DOM can be hard work for the browser. If you're not careful, things can get very sluggish very quickly. But if there's a whole class of script that isn't allowed access to the DOM, then the browser can happily run that script in parallel to its regular rendering activities, safe in the knowledge that it's an entirely separate process.

The first kind of script to come with this constraint was called a *web worker*. In a web worker, you could write some JavaScript to do number-crunching calculations without slowing down whatever else was being displayed in the browser window. Spin up a web worker to generate larger and larger prime numbers, for instance, and it will merrily do so in the background.

A service worker is like a web worker with extra powers. It still can't access the DOM, but it does have access to the fundamental inner workings of the browser.

Browsers and servers

Let's take a step back and think about how the World Wide Web works. It's a beautiful ballet of client and server. The client is usually a web browser—or, to use the parlance of web standards, a *user agent*: a piece of software that acts on behalf of the user.

The user wants to accomplish a task or find some information. The URL is the key technology that will empower the user in their quest. They will either type a URL into their web browser or follow a link to get there. This is the point at which the web browser—or client—makes a request to a web server. Before the request can reach the server, it must traverse the internet of undersea cables, radio towers, and even the occasional satellite (**FIG 1.1**).

Imagine if you could leave instructions for the web browser that would be executed *before the request is even sent*. That's exactly what service workers allow you to do (**FIG 1.2**).

Usually when we write JavaScript, the code is executed after it's been downloaded from a server. With service workers, we can write a script that's executed by the browser before anything else happens. We can tell the browser, "If the user asks you to retrieve a URL for this particular website, run this corresponding bit of JavaScript first." That explains why service workers don't have access to the Document Object Model; when the service worker is run, there's no document yet.

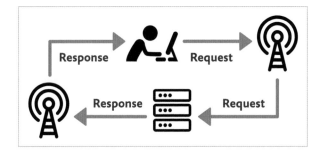

FIG 1.1: Browsers send URL requests to servers, and servers respond by sending files.

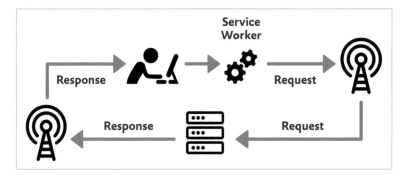

FIG 1.2: Service workers tell the web browser to do something *before* they send the request to queue up a URL.

Getting your head around service workers

A service worker is like a cookie. Cookies are downloaded from a web server and installed in a browser. You can go to your browser's preferences and see all the cookies that have been installed by sites you've visited. Cookies are very small and very simple little text files. A website can set a cookie, read a cookie, and update a cookie. A service worker script is much more powerful. It contains a set of instructions that the browser will consult before making any requests to the site that originally installed the service worker.

A service worker is like a virus. When you visit a website, a service worker is surreptitiously installed in the background. Afterwards, whenever you make a request to that website, your request will be intercepted by the service worker first. Your computer or phone becomes the home for service workers lurking in wait, ready to perform man-in-the-middle attacks. Don't panic. A service worker can only handle requests for the site that originally installed that service worker. When you write a service worker, you can only use it to perform man-in-the-middle attacks on your own website.

A service worker is like a toolbox. By itself, a service worker can't do much. But it allows you to access some very powerful browser features, like the Fetch API, the Cache API, and even notifications. API stands for *Application Programming Interface*, which sounds very fancy but really just means a tool that you can program however you want. You can write a set of instructions in your service worker to take advantage of these tools. Most of your instructions will be written as "when this happens, reach for this tool." If, for instance, the network connection fails, you can instruct the service worker to retrieve a backup file using the Cache API.

A service worker is like a duck-billed platypus. The platypus not only lactates, but also lays eggs. It's the only mammal capable of making its own custard. A service worker can also... Actually, hang on, a service worker is nothing like a duck-billed platypus! Sorry about that. But a service worker is somewhat like a cookie, and somewhat like a virus, and somewhat like a toolbox.

SAFETY FIRST

SERVICE WORKERS ARE POWERFUL. Once a service worker has been installed on your machine, it lies in wait, like a patient spider waiting to feel the vibrations of a particular thread.

Imagine if a malicious ne'er-do-well wanted to wreak havoc by impersonating a website in order to install a service worker. They could write instructions in the service worker to prevent the website ever appearing in that browser again. Or they could write instructions to swap out the content displayed under that site's domain. That's why it's so important to make sure that a service worker really belongs to the site it claims to come from. As the specification for service workers puts it, they "create the opportunity for a bad actor to turn a bad day into a bad eternity (http://bkaprt.com/go/01-01/)." To prevent this calamity, service workers require you to adhere to two policies:

1) Same origin.
2) HTTPS only.

The same-origin policy means that a website at example.com can only install a service worker script that lives at example.com. That means you can't put your service worker script on a different domain. You can use a domain like s3.amazonaws.com for hosting your images and other assets, but not your service worker script. That domain wouldn't match the domain of the site installing the service worker.

The HTTPS-only policy means that https://example.com can install a service worker, but http://example.com can't. A site running under HTTPS (the S stands for *Secure*) instead of HTTP is much harder to spoof. Without HTTPS, the communication between a browser and a server could be intercepted and altered. If you're sitting in a coffee shop with an open Wi-Fi network, there's no guarantee that anything you're reading in browser from http://newswebsite.com hasn't been tampered with. But if you're reading something from https://newswebsite.com, you can be pretty sure you're getting what you asked for.

Securing your site

Enabling HTTPS on your site opens up a whole series of secure-only browser features—like the JavaScript APIs for geolocation, payments, notifications, and service workers. Even if you never plan to add a service worker to your site, it's still a good idea to switch to HTTPS. A secure connection makes it trickier for snoopers to see who's visiting which websites. Your website might not contain particularly sensitive information, but when someone visits your site, that's between you and your visitor. Enabling HTTPS won't stop unethical surveillance by the NSA, but it makes the surveillance slightly more difficult.

There's one exception. You can use a service worker on a site being served from `localhost`, a web server on your own computer, not part of the web. That means you can play around with service workers without having to deploy your code to a live site every time you want to test something.

If you're using a Mac, you can spin up a local server from the command line. Let's say your website is in a folder called `mysite`. Drag that folder to the Terminal app, or open up the Terminal app and navigate to that folder using the `cd` command to change directory. Then type:

```
python -m SimpleHTTPServer 8000
```

This starts a web server from the `mysite` folder, served over port 8000. Now you can visit localhost:8000 in a web browser on the same computer, which means you can add a service worker to the website you've got inside the `mysite` folder: http://localhost:8000.

But if you then put the site live at, say, http://mysite.com, the service worker won't run. You'll need to serve the site from https://mysite.com instead. To do that, you need a secure certificate for your server.

There was a time when certificates cost money and were difficult to install. Now, thanks to a service called Certbot, certificates are free. But I'm not going to lie: it still feels a bit intimidating to install the certificate. There's something about logging on to a server and typing commands that makes me simultaneously feel like a l33t hacker, and also like I'm going to break everything. Fortunately, the process of using Certbot is relatively jargon-free (**FIG 1.3**).

On the Certbot website (http://bkaprt.com/go/01-02/), you choose which kind of web server and operating system your site is running on. From there you'll be guided step-by-step through the commands you need to type in the command line of your web server's computer, which means you'll need to have SSH access to that machine. If you're on shared hosting,

FIG 1.3: The website of EFF's Certbot.

that might not be possible. In that case, check to see if your hosting provider offers secure certificates. If not, please pester them to do so, or switch to a hosting provider that can serve your site over HTTPS.

Another option is to stay with your current hosting provider, but use a service like Cloudflare to act as a "front" for your website. These services can serve your website's files from data centers around the world, making sure that the physical distance between your site's visitors and your site's files is nice and short. And while they're at it, these services can make sure all of those files are served over HTTPS.

Once you're set up with HTTPS, you're ready to write a service worker script. It's time to open up your favorite text editor. You're about to turbocharge your website!

2
PREPARING FOR OFFLINE

BEFORE YOU EXPEND ENERGY creating a service worker script, you might be wondering if it's worth the investment. You probably want to know which browsers support service workers, and by extension, how many of your site's visitors will benefit from this technology.

You can go to caniuse.com and find the current support levels for service workers (FIG 2.1). At the time of writing, it's not exactly a field of green. Quite a few of the major browsers support service workers, but there are some glaring omissions. Some of the visitors to your website are almost certainly using browsers that don't support service workers.

You could wait until just about every browser ships support for service workers before adding this technology to your site. Though, fortunately, because of the way service workers have been designed, you don't have to wait. You can deploy a service worker to your site today. The supporting browsers will get the benefit, and the non-supporting browsers will carry on just as they do right now. Think of your service worker as a reward for users of more modern browsers. Crucially, you won't be punishing users of less modern browsers.

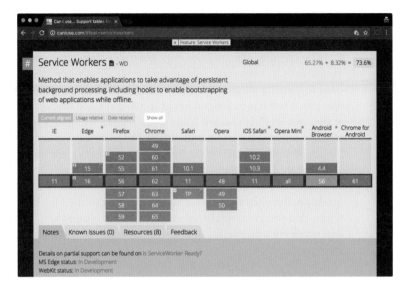

FIG 2.1: You can find current browser support for service workers at https://caniuse.com.

Before a service worker can be installed on a user's machine, they must first visit your website. For that first visit, there's no service worker, regardless of whether the user's browser has support for service workers or not. When it comes to first-time visits, no browser can benefit from a service worker. That means a service worker can only be deployed as an enhancement. Even if you wanted to make a website that relied completely on a service worker, that first visit would foil your fiendish plan.

I think that's a brilliant piece of design. Because service workers must be applied as an extra layer on top of your existing functionality, the levels of support on caniuse.com really don't matter. Even if only one browser supported service workers, it would still be worth adding one to your site. Best of all, as more and more browsers add support for service workers, more and more people will benefit from the work you do today.

REGISTRATION

Start by creating a blank JavaScript file called `serviceworker.js` and save it in the same folder as your website. You might be used to putting all your JavaScript files into their own folder, like `/js/`, but I recommend keeping your service worker file at the root level. If you put it somewhere else, things get complicated when it comes to which URLs the service worker can intercept. Putting your service worker file at `/serviceworker.js` keeps things simple.

Before the service worker can be installed on a visitor's machine, the visitor's browser needs to know of the file's existence. You need to point to the service worker file and say, "See that service worker script over there? Install it, please." This is called *registration*.

The simplest way to do this is with a `link` element in the head of your site's HTML:

```
<link rel="serviceworker" href="/serviceworker.js">
```

Alas, we can't rely on this just yet. At the time of writing, not many browsers support this nice declarative way of pointing to service worker scripts. But that's okay. We can still use JavaScript. You can put this JavaScript in an external file or put it at the bottom of your HTML:

```
<script>
navigator.serviceWorker.register('/serviceworker.
  js');
</script>
```

This highlights an interesting difference between HTML and JavaScript. If a browser doesn't support service workers, and you present it with the `link rel="serviceworker"` element, the browser will ignore it. That's down to the error-handling model of HTML—it ignores what it doesn't understand. That can be frustrating if you're trying to debug HTML. If you make a typo, the browser won't complain—it will simply ignore it. But it's a powerful feature when it comes to extending the language. New elements, attributes, and `rel` values can be added to HTML, safe in the knowledge that older browsers will quietly ignore them and move on. That's not how browsers behave with JavaScript. If you give a browser some JavaScript it doesn't understand, it will throw an error. Worse, the browser will stop parsing that block of JavaScript. Any subsequent code, even if it's error-free, will never get executed.

If you point a browser at a service worker script using JavaScript, but that browser doesn't understand what you mean by `navigator.serviceWorker`, it won't just ignore what you've written—it will throw an error.

Feature detection

There's a way around this. Before using a browser feature in JavaScript, you can ask the browser whether or not the feature exists. This is imaginatively called *feature detection*.

You can apply feature detection to just about anything that's available through JavaScript. If you wanted to use the Geolocation API, your feature detection might look like this:

```
if (navigator.geolocation) {
  // Your code goes here
}
```

That line beginning with `//` is a comment. It won't be executed by the browser. It's not meant for machines; it's meant for humans. Comments are a great way of leaving reminders for your future self, like Guy Pearce in *Memento* or Arnold Schwarzenegger in *Total Recall*.

The comment is there for you. The `if` statement is there for the browser. The `if` statement checks to see if there's such a thing as a `geolocation` property in the `navigator` object.

Wait a minute. Objects? Properties? What is this moon language I'm suddenly spouting?

An object lesson

For the longest time, I was intimidated by concepts like Object-Oriented Programming. Not only was it written in capital letters to demonstrate its seriousness, it also had its own vocabulary of terms. I knew some JavaScript, so I knew what a *variable* was (a label for storing a value—the value can change, but the label stays the same), and I knew what a *function* was (a block of code that can be executed by invoking its label), but I had no idea what a *property* or a *method* was.

Imagine my surprise when I found out that a property is just another name for a variable, and a method is just another name for a function. The only difference is that properties and methods have a parent, called an *object*—not exactly a very revealing name (we're lucky we didn't up with Thing-Oriented Programming).

Properties and methods are preceded by the parent's label and a dot:

```
object.property
object.method()
```

Web browsers expose their features to JavaScript through objects. There's one parent object called `window`. That object contains other objects, chained together with dots. The `document` object belongs to the `window` object:

```
window.document
```

So does the `navigator` object:

```
window.navigator
```

So `document` and `navigator` are properties of the `window` object, as well as being objects themselves.

The `window` object is so ubiquitous that you don't even have to specify it if you don't want to. That's handy because `document` and `navigator` can have their own objects, which in turn have their own properties and methods. It can get quite long-winded to write:

```
window.navigator.serviceWorker.register();
```

You can save a bit of space by writing:

```
navigator.serviceWorker.register();
```

That's the `register` method of the `serviceWorker` object: the `serviceWorker` object is a property of the `navigator` object (which is in turn a property of the `window` object). You can read it backwards from right to left, substituting each dot for the words "belongs to": `register` belongs to `serviceWorker`, which belongs to `navigator` (which belongs to `window`).

The property test

With feature detection, you're checking for the existence of properties. If you want to use service workers, you can first ask the browser if there's a property called `serviceWorker` that belongs to the `navigator` object:

```
if (navigator.serviceWorker) {
  // Your code goes here
}
```

In an older browser that doesn't support service workers, `navigator.serviceWorker` returns a value of `undefined`—there's no such property. In a newer browser, `navigator.serviceWorker` exists and is an object.

There are many ways to do feature detection. You could use the `in` operator to rifle through the `navigator` object looking for the `serviceWorker` property:

```
if ('serviceWorker' in navigator) {
  // Your code goes here
}
```

Or you could explicitly check that the serviceWorker object doesn't have a value of undefined:

```
if (navigator.serviceWorker !== undefined) {
  // Your code goes here
}
```

Whichever way you decide to apply feature detection, it's always a good idea to do it before using a browser feature. With this in mind, here's how you can point to your service worker file from your HTML:

```
<script>
if (navigator.serviceWorker) {
  navigator.serviceWorker.register('/serviceworker.
  js');
}
</script>
```

Now you're safely running the register method of the serviceWorker object, secure in the knowledge that nonsupporting browsers will never try to execute that code.

Whenever I see that something is a method, I do a little mental substitution—replacing the word *method* with the word *function*—to remind myself how methods work. The parentheses after the name of the method are a dead giveaway that methods work just like functions (they just happen to be functions that belong to a parent object).

The parentheses are where we can pass in values to a function—or to a method. For some reason, these values are known as *arguments*. I have no idea why this is. It makes talking about code sound quite confrontational: "Pass these arguments into this method" sounds like an instruction to pick a fight.

In the case of the register method, you're currently passing in one argument—the URL of your service worker script:

```
register(url)
```

The value of that URL will define the scope of the service worker—how much of your site the service worker will control.

Scope

By default, the scope is derived from where you put your service worker script. If your service worker script resides at /js/ serviceworker.js, the script will only be able to control URLs that start with /js.

There might be situations when you want the same domain to have multiple service workers, such as /myapp/service-worker1.js and /myotherapp/serviceworker2.js. Because the scope of a service worker is defined by its URL, you can point to both of them from anywhere in your site:

```
navigator.serviceWorker.register('/myapp/
  serviceworker1.js');
navigator.serviceWorker.register('/myotherapp/
  serviceworker2.js');
```

The first service worker will have control over /myapp/. The second service worker will have control over /myotherapp/.

What if you have one service worker for the whole site, but another one for a specific folder?

```
navigator.serviceWorker.register('/serviceworker1.
  js');
navigator.serviceWorker.register('/myapp/
  serviceworker2.js');
```

First you're declaring that one service worker should have control over every URL, then you're declaring that another service worker should have control over certain URLs. Which declaration wins?

There's a fairly simple formula for figuring that out: the service worker script with the longest path in its URL will win. The service worker inside myapp will handle any requests that start with /myapp/. Every other URL will be handled by / serviceworker1.js.

Another option is to put all your service worker scripts at the root level, and then declare the scope from JavaScript. Let's say your scripts are /serviceworker1.js and /serviceworker2.js. The first service worker script is for the whole site, so you can point to it like this:

```
navigator.serviceWorker.register('/serviceworker1.
  js');
```

The other service worker script is only intended for /myapp/. You can declare this by passing in another argument to the register method:

```
navigator.serviceWorker.register('/serviceworker2.
  js', {
  scope: '/myapp/'
});
```

The declarative equivalent of this—once browsers support it—will be:

```
<link rel="serviceworker" href="/serviceworker1.js">
<link rel="serviceworker" href="/serviceworker2.js"
  scope="/myapp/">
```

While it's good to know how to set the scope of different service workers, most websites will only ever have one service worker responsible for the whole site.

The register method lives up to its name. You're asking the browser to register the existence of a service worker script. Your code should look something like this:

```
if (navigator.serviceWorker) {
  navigator.serviceWorker.register('/serviceworker.
    js');
}
```

PROMISES

When you ask the browser to register the existence of your service worker script, you're going to have to give it a few moments. First, the browser needs to verify that the current site is either running on HTTPS or `localhost`. Then, it needs to check that the service worker script is on the same domain as the current site. Finally, the browser will attempt to fetch the service worker script and parse it.

None of these steps will take very long, but you wouldn't want the browser to freeze while it's busy with these tasks. That's why the `register` method is executed asynchronously. The browser doesn't finish executing the `register` method before moving on to the next line of code. Instead, it moves straight on to the next line of code while it carries out its tasks in the background.

That's great for browser performance, but what if we want to give the browser some further instructions once the `register` method has finished its chores?

The old way of executing the extra instructions would involve listening out for events—maybe something like `load` or `ready`. That works, but it can result in code that's hard to read. There's another way of handling asynchronous events that results in more elegant code: promises.

A *promise* is a kind of object that comes with a built-in method called `then`. Whatever function you put inside the `then` method will only be executed when the promise has successfully finished all its tasks. At this point, we say that the promise has been fulfilled, much like the closing chapter of a revenge thriller or the denouement to a fairy tale.

```
promise
.then( function () {
  // Yay! It worked.
});
```

If something goes wrong along the way and the promise isn't fulfilled, there's a corresponding `catch` method. You can put a function in there to make amends for the unsuccessful fulfillment of the promise. The end result looks something like this:

```
promise
.then( function () {
  // Yay! It worked.
})
.catch( function () {
  // Boo! It failed.
});
```

You don't have to put the `then` and `catch` methods on new lines like that. That's just my preference. You might prefer to write:

```
promise.then(
  function () {
    // Yay! It worked.
  }
).catch(
  function () {
    // Boo! It failed.
  }
);
```

You could even write the whole thing on one line if you want to be the James Joyce of JavaScript.

In those examples, the functions inside `then` and `catch` are anonymous functions. That doesn't mean that they're ashamed of anything they're doing; it means that they don't have names. They're created on the fly and then never referred to again. You don't have to use anonymous functions. You could invoke functions that you've written elsewhere—functions that are proud of their names, not hiding behind the veil of anonymity:

```
promise
.then(doSomething)
.catch(doSomethingElse);
```

If I were the judgmental sort, I would have to say that doSomething and doSomethingElse aren't names to be proud of, but the point is they can be reused. And if you use them within then or catch you know that they won't run until the promise is fulfilled or rejected. That's right—we call it a *rejection* when a promise isn't fulfilled.

Promises, fulfillments, and rejections—this is beginning to feel like a soap opera.

The order of events

Promises are perfect for asynchronous tasks. Registering a service worker is an asynchronous task. Let's prove it. Try out this piece of code:

```
<script>
if (navigator.serviceWorker) {
  navigator.serviceWorker.register('/serviceworker.
  js')
  .then( function () {
    console.log('Success!');
  })
  .catch( function () {
    console.error('Failure!');
  });
  console.log('All done.');
}
</script>
```

Add that JavaScript to the bottom of your HTML page, reload the page in a web browser, then open up the browser's JavaScript console (alt+cmd+j). Here's what you should see:

```
All done.
Success!
```

Unless something went horribly wrong, in which case you'll see:

```
All done.
Failure!
```

Notice that the command to log "All done." was at the end of your code, and yet it's the first log command to get executed. Usually JavaScript code is executed in a procedural way—the order in which commands are given is also the order in which those commands are executed. Asynchronous commands—like `serviceWorker.register`—will finish executing in their own good time. That's asynchronousness... asynchronicity... asynchronaciousness... that's how this kind of thing works.

Winning arguments

When a promise is fulfilled (or rejected), it can send data to the function that's waiting patiently inside `then` (or `catch`). To access that data, you'll need to include it as an argument inside the waiting function. Here's an example:

```
navigator.serviceWorker.register('/serviceworker.
  js')
.then( function (registration) {
  console.log('success!', registration.scope);
});
```

In this case, I'm passing the data from successful registration in a variable called `registration`. That data is an object. I'm then accessing the `scope` property of that object. That gives me something like:

```
Success! http://localhost:8000/
```

That word `registration` is just what I'm calling the object being returned from a successful service worker registration. I could call it anything—for instance, this code works exactly the same way:

```
navigator.serviceWorker.register('/serviceworker.
  js')
.then( function (x) {
  console.log('success!', x.scope);
});
```

Whenever you receive data from a promise, you can call it anything you want. Personally, I think that `registration` makes more sense than x because it describes the data better.

A promise can also pass data to the function within `catch`. That's really useful for debugging. Here's an example where I'm deliberately going to cause an error by trying to point to a non-existent service worker file:

```
navigator.serviceWorker.register('/nothing.js')
.catch( function (error) {
  console.error('Failure!', error);
});
```

Now I'll see something like this in the console:

```
Failure! TypeError: Failed to register a
  ServiceWorker: A bad HTTP response code (404) was
  received when fetching the script.
```

Again, that name `error` is just my name for the data. I could've called it x or y or anything:

```
navigator.serviceWorker.register('/nothing.js')
.catch( function (y) {
  console.error('Failure!', y);
});
```

Feel free to update the JavaScript code in your HTML to take advantage of the data being passed in from the `regis-ter` promise:

```
<script>
if (navigator.serviceWorker) {
  navigator.serviceWorker.register('/serviceworker.
  js')
  .then( function (registration) {
    console.log('Success!', registration.scope);
  })
  .catch( function (error) {
    console.error('Failure!', error);
  });
}
</script>
```

Looking good. You're practicing feature detection, you're handling promises, and most important, you're registering a service worker for your site. But that service worker isn't doing anything yet. It's just a blank file.

Let's fix that.

3 MAKING FETCH HAPPEN

RIGHT NOW, YOUR SERVICE WORKER FILE IS EMPTY. An empty service worker file won't do anything by default. That might sound obvious, but it's a very deliberate design decision. There are plenty of technologies that try to anticipate your needs and provide you with default behaviors without you having to specify anything. That sounds great—unless those default behaviors are not what you wanted.

I realize I'm being quite vague, so I'll be more specific. But I warn you, I am about to drag some skeletons from the darkest depths of the browser and out into the light. Huddle a little closer to the campfire, and I'll position this flashlight under my chin while I tell you a tale...

THE EXTENSIBLE WEB

What if I told you that service workers aren't the first technology to enable websites to work offline? There was a previous attempt to solve the offline problem using a technology called Application Cache, or AppCache for short. If you haven't heard of AppCache, that's good. We try not to speak its name. Those poor unfortunate souls who dabbled too deep in the dark arts of AppCache have banished it from their minds, lest they be driven out of their wits by such painful memories.

AppCache was forged in the fires of the standards process, hidden from the gaze of mortal web developers. The spec was then triumphantly unveiled. "Behold!" cried the standard bearers, "We've given you a way to make your sites work offline!" Web developers eagerly took hold of this new knowledge, implemented AppCache, and promptly broke their websites.

It all looked so good on paper (and on mailing list). You created a new file called an *application manifest*. In that manifest, you listed which files should be cached. From then on, the listed files would always be retrieved from the cache instead of from the network.

It seemed straightforward enough, but the devil was in the details. In order to tell the browser where the manifest file lived, you needed to point to it using a manifest attribute in your document's `html` element. As soon as you did that, the HTML file was automatically added to the list of files to be cached. It didn't matter if you updated the HTML—your users would still see the stale version from the cache. Trying to break this stranglehold on your site meant entering a painful world of cache invalidation. It was a mess.

AppCache sounded great in theory, but fell apart in practice. In retrospect, the root of the problem seems obvious. Instead of consulting with developers on the functionality they wanted, the spec was created by imagining what developers wanted. It makes more sense to give developers the tools they need to create their own offline solutions, than giving them an inflexible technology that only works in limited situations.

Giving developers access to the building blocks they need to craft their own solutions is the driving force behind an idea called *the extensible web*. There's even a manifesto:

Our primary goal is to tighten the feedback loop between the editors of web standards and web developers. We prefer an evolutionary model of standardization, driven by the vast army

of web developers, to a top-down model of progress driven by
standardization. (http://bkaprt.com/go/03-01/)

Stirring stuff. It makes me want to storm the barricades (and replace them with well-designed, standardized barricades). Whereas AppCache added a layer of "magic" on top of the work the browser was doing under the hood, service workers expose the true inner workings of the browser.

Browser vendors should provide new low-level capabilities that
expose the possibilities of the underlying platform as closely as
possible. (http://bkaprt.com/go/03-01/)

Developers then have to provide step-by-step instructions to browsers detailing exactly what we want to happen. That's more work than the straightforward, declarative approach of AppCache, but it's also more empowering. Writing JavaScript is the price we pay for these newfound powers.

That's why your service worker file isn't doing anything yet. You need to fill it with instructions first. That means you need to decide what you want your service worker to do.

EVENTS

An empty service worker file won't do anything, but it still gets installed on the user's machine. You can see this for yourself by looking in your browser's development tools. I recommend using Chrome for this. Visit the local version of your site—the one with the service worker registration code in the HTML—and open up Developer Tools (alt+cmd+i). Click on the Application panel. Then, from the menu in the sidebar, select Service Workers (**FIG 3.1**).

This shows that a service worker has been activated, like a sleeper agent in a Cold War thriller. Now it's time to add some JavaScript to that empty service worker file, serviceworker.js.

When you write JavaScript that's going to be executed by a web browser, it often follows this pattern:

FIG 3.1: The Service Workers section in Chrome's Developer Tools (under the Application panel).

1) When this event happens,
   a) do something.

The event you're listening out for could be triggered by the user—clicking, scrolling, or hovering, for instance. You can then use that event as your cue to do something—show some information, trigger an animation, or make an Ajax request to the server.

It's a similar situation with service workers. You can still write code that listens for events, but this time the events are triggered by the browser itself as it goes about its business. The way that a browser works its magic is through the fetch event.

When you click on a link or type a URL into the browser's address bar, that triggers the fetch event—the browser will "fetch" that document from the web. If that HTML document has images in it, each img element will trigger another fetch event—the browser will "fetch" the files referenced in the src attributes. If the page links to a stylesheet with rel="-stylesheet", that will also trigger a fetch event. The same goes for a JavaScript file referenced from the src attribute of a script element.

In your service worker script, you can listen for every single one of those fetch events. You can use addEventListener to do this:

FIG 3.2: The Service Workers section of the Application panel in Chrome's Developer Tools shows that the old service worker is still in control.

```
addEventListener('fetch', function (event) {
  console.log('The service worker is listening.');
});
```

This is following the familiar pattern of listening for an event, and then executing some code when the event is triggered:

1) Whenever a `fetch` event happens,
   a) log this message to the browser console.

In the settings for the Console panel in Chrome's DevTools, tick the "Preserve log" option—that way you'll get a record of every `fetch` event. Save the changes you've made in the `serviceworker.js` file and reload the page in your browser. If you look in the Console panel of DevTools, you'll see...nothing new. What's going on? Why doesn't it say, "The service worker is listening."?

The key to unravelling this mystery is to look in the Application panel again. The status message now shows two service workers. When you edited the service worker script, the browser saw that as being a whole new service worker. It can't swap out the existing service worker for the new one just yet, because the page currently loaded in the browser is still under the control of the original service worker (**FIG 3.2**).

THE SERVICE WORKER LIFE CYCLE

Let's back up for a moment and think about all the steps involved in getting a service worker up and running.

The whole process starts with registration, which you initiated from a `script` element in your HTML:

```
navigator.serviceWorker.register('/serviceworker.
    js');
```

The service worker file is downloaded. After download comes installation. This is followed by activation, when the service worker takes control of this particular browser. After activation, every request to your site will be routed through the service worker.

The first time a browser visits your site, the life cycle of the service worker seems straightforward enough:

1. Download
2. Install
3. Activate

When you update your service worker script, you aren't updating the service worker that's been installed on the user's machine. Instead, you're creating a whole new service worker. This new service worker is downloaded and installed, but it isn't automatically activated. The new service worker is waiting in the wings, ready to be activated, but as long as the user is navigating around your site, the old service worker is still in charge.

The way that service workers get updated is similar to the way that browsers themselves get updated. If there's a new version of Chrome, it gets downloaded in the background. But Chrome doesn't restart without asking. Instead, it waits until you shut down the browser. Only then does it install the new version of the browser and delete the old one.

FIG 3.3: A service worker with a numeric ID is running.

It's the same with service workers—the update is downloaded in the background, but it doesn't take effect until the browser is closed and reopened. Until then, it's waiting.

So the life cycle for an updated service worker is more like this:

1. Download
2. Install
3. **Wait**
4. Activate

The new service worker will patiently wait until the user has the left your website. As long as the user has a single browser tab open with your website in it, the old service worker is active.

You can see the service worker life cycle in action using the Developer Tools in Chrome. Under the Service Workers section in the Application panel, you'll see which service worker is currently active (**FIG 3.3**). It will have a unique number. The Status will say something like "#12345 is activated and is running."

When you update your service worker script, a new service worker with a new number will appear, saying something like "#12346 is waiting to activate" (**FIG 3.4**).

FIG 3.4: Another service worker with a different numeric ID is waiting to take over.

Updating your service worker

As long as you have a browser window or tab open with a domain that's under the control of a service worker, the new version of that service worker has to wait in the wings. This can make debugging quite tricky. If you have multiple browser windows or tabs open, you need to make sure that you haven't accidentally left one running with the old service worker in control, or none of them will get the updated service worker.

There are two things you can do to make sure the updated service worker kicks in. You can either shut down any browser windows or tabs that have `localhost` loaded in them, or you can use the handy `skipWaiting` command in the Application panel in DevTools. Then, the next time you load the page, the new service worker will be activated and the old one will fade away into oblivion.

Now when you reload the page, you'll finally be greeted with this message in your browser console:

```
The service worker is listening.
```

When you're working with service workers, you may find yourself refreshing your browser window many times. It's important to note that if you do a hard refresh—pressing Shift while you refresh—you'll bypass the service worker completely.

If you like, you can see the service worker installation and activation in action by listening to the `install` and `activate` events:

```
addEventListener('install', function (event) {
  console.log('The service worker is
  installing...');
});

addEventListener('activate', function (event) {
  console.log('The service worker is activated.');
});

addEventListener('fetch', function (event) {
  console.log('The service worker is listening.');
});
```

Save those changes in your `serviceworker.js` file. Once again, if you refresh your browser window, you won't see any changes; your new service worker script is waiting to take effect while your page is still in the clutches of the old version. Close your browser window, or use the `skipWaiting` link in DevTools. Now when you reopen a browser window and navigate to your local site, you'll see these messages:

```
The service worker is installing...
The service worker is activated.
```

As long as your browser window is open, you won't see either message again. But every time you refresh the page, you'll trigger a new `fetch` event:

```
The service worker is listening.
```

THE fetch EVENT

When you intercept a `fetch` event, you can do whatever you want with the data being passed into the anonymous function you've created. The data is available through the event argument you're passing into that function:

```
addEventListener('fetch', function (event) {
  // Do something with 'event' data
});
```

You don't have to call it event. You could call it x, y, or z if you wanted:

```
addEventListener('fetch', function (z) {
  // Do something with 'z' data
});
```

I find it's useful to use a descriptive word like fetchEvent or event (or even just evt, as long as your future self can remember what it's short for). It's your code, so you can use whatever makes sense to you.

```
addEventListener('fetch', function (fetchEvent) {
  // Do something with 'fetchEvent' data
});
```

Something else you can do is use some of the fancy new JavaScript syntax that was added in ES6. I know it would make more sense if it were called JS6, but why keep things logical when they can be deliberately obscure and confusing?

One of the new syntax features is designed to remove those ugly anonymous function declarations and replace them with ASCII art in the shape of an arrow:

```
addEventListener('fetch', fetchEvent => {
  // Do something with 'fetchEvent' data
});
```

I quite like the way those new arrow functions look. Again, it's your code so use whichever syntax makes most sense to you.

Usually I'm cautious about using new JavaScript syntax in web browsers. If a browser doesn't understand the new syntax, it will throw an error and stop parsing the script. But that's not going to happen inside a service worker script. Every browser that supports service workers also supports the new ES6 features. Your service worker script is a safe space for you to dabble with new syntax.

Other new additions to the JavaScript language are `let` and `const`. Previously we had to use `var` to create all our variables:

```
addEventListener('fetch', fetchEvent => {
  var request = fetchEvent.request;
});
```

Now we can use `let` for variables that will change value, and `const` for variables that should remain constant:

```
addEventListener('fetch', event => {
  const request = fetchEvent.request;
});
```

In this case, you're creating a variable called `request`, just so you don't have to keep typing `fetchEvent.request` every time you want to examine that property.

If you output the contents of `request`, you'll see quite a bit of data (**FIG 3.5**):

```
addEventListener('fetch', fetchEvent => {
  const request = fetchEvent.request;
  console.log(request);
});
```

Remember, you'll need to close down your browser tab or use the `skipWaiting` link in the Application panel of Chrome's Developer Tools to apply your changes. If you don't see the `skipWaiting` link, you can also use the `Unregister` link to delete the current service worker. Refreshing the page should install the new service worker. Refreshing the page again will allow that service worker to listen to `fetch` events and log its data.

FIG 3.5: The Console panel in Chrome's Developer Tools showing the details of a request.

In the JavaScript console, you'll see a `Request` object with all sorts of properties: `method`, `mode`, `referrer`, `credentials`, and `url`—that's the URL of the file that's being fetched. All of that scrumptious information will come in handy later.

Intercepting `fetch` events

Until now you've been observing the `fetch` events that the browser is carrying out. The real power comes with altering those events.

Using `respondWith`, you can send back your own custom response. You can create a new `Response` object and put anything you like in it:

```
addEventListener('fetch', fetchEvent => {
  fetchEvent.respondWith(
    new Response('Hello, world!')
  ); // end respondWith
}); // end addEventListener
```

You'll need to do the dance of deletion in the DevTools Application panel to see the fruits of your labor. Once your new service worker is installed, every request it intercepts will result in a page saying, "Hello, world!" and nothing else. That's a terrible user experience, but it illustrates the power you can wield within service workers.

THE FETCH API

The Fetch API allows you as a developer to instruct the browser to fetch any resources you want, effectively recreating what the browser is doing. Granted, there's not much point in doing this other than to demonstrate how much control you now have at your command. Later you'll be able to use this superpower to optimize your site.

Fetching resources is an asynchronous activity, so the Fetch API uses promises like this:

```
fetch(request)
.then( responseFromFetch => {
  // Success!
})
.catch( error => {
  // Failure!
});
```

You can create a fetch event inside your service worker by using respondWith:

```
addEventListener('fetch', fetchEvent => {
  const request = fetchEvent.request;
  fetchEvent.respondWith(
    fetch(request)
    .then( responseFromFetch => {
      return responseFromFetch;
    }) // end fetch then
  ); // end respondWith
}); // end addEventListener
```

That code is telling the browser to do what it would do anyway: fetch a resource, and return with the contents of that resource.

Now you can go one step further: you can tell the browser what to do if the request for that resource doesn't succeed. That's what the catch clause is for. You can create a custom response in there:

```
addEventListener('fetch', fetchEvent => {
  const request = fetchEvent.request;
  fetchEvent.respondWith(
    fetch(request)
    .then(responseFromFetch => {
      return responseFromFetch;
    }) // end fetch then
    .catch(error => {
      return new Response('Oops! Something went
wrong.');
    }) // end fetch catch
  ); // end respondWith
}); // end addEventListener
```

To test whether or not this is working, you'll first have to update your service worker—do the Unregister, Reload, Reload samba in the Application panel—then take your browser offline. There's a quick way to do this that doesn't involve switching off your Wi-Fi or unplugging your ethernet cable: in the Service Workers panel of the Application panel in Chrome Developer Tools, there's a checkbox labeled Offline. If you check this, it does exactly what it says on the tin—your browser is effectively offline. Reload the page while this checkbox is ticked, and you'll see the response you crafted:

```
Oops! Something went wrong.
```

It's not the most informative of messages, but it demonstrates that you're no longer at the mercy of the browser's default offline message.

Try refining your offline message by adding some HTML:

```
return new Response('<h1>Oops!</h1> <p>Something
    went wrong.</p>');
```

Update the service worker in the Application panel using `skipWaiting`, but don't forget to untick the Offline option before doing that. Then, when the new service worker is installed, try going offline again. This time you'll see a different message:

```
<h1>Oops!</h1> <p>Something went wrong.</p>
```

That's not quite right. We don't want to see those HTML undergarments.

The message is being sent as plain text instead of HTML. You can fix that by passing in a second argument to the `Response` object where you can specify the headers:

```
return new Response(
    '<h1>Oops!</h1> <p>Something went wrong.</p>',
    {
        headers: {'Content-type': 'text/html;
        charset=utf-8'}
    }
);
```

Untick the Offline checkbox and update the service worker. Once the new service worker is up and running, tick that Offline option again and reload. This time you will see glorious HTML (**FIG 3.6**).

This is working nicely, but it isn't going to scale if you want to provide a nicer offline experience. Writing an entire HTML page inside your service worker script doesn't seem right. You'll also probably want your offline page to have images and other assets. It would be better if you could make a standalone offline page, get the service worker to store it, and later display it whenever the user is offline. What you need is the power of caching.

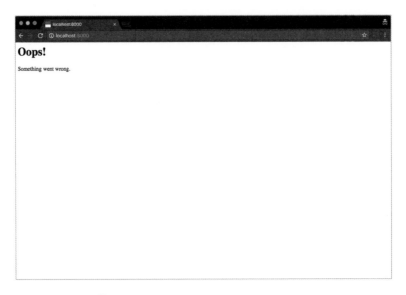

FIG 3.6: A custom offline message.

4 CACHE ME IF YOU CAN

WHEN THE WEB WAS CREATED, it had no memory. I don't mean memory in the sense of kilobytes, megabytes, and gigabytes; I mean memory in the literal sense.

As you'll recall from Chapter 1, a web browser requests a page from a web server. The server sends a response. This might be the first time that this particular browser has interacted with this particular server, or it might be the hundredth time. Without any memory of one another, they can never form a lasting relationship. Every time is just like the first time.

Because the word *memory* is already taken, we use the word *state* to describe these situations. A system that can retain knowledge of previous interactions is *stateful*. At its outset, the web was *stateless*.

Managing state can be tricky. The fact that the web was stateless kept it nice and simple. Anybody creating a new browser or new server software didn't have to worry about the arrow of time. But the stateless nature of the web was also frustrating. If you were trying to build a business on the web, you had no way of forming a relationship with your customers.

Imagine a user adding a product to their shopping cart, clicking on a link to another product, and finding their shopping cart empty again as though the past had never happened. An engineer at Netscape named Lou Montulli created cookies to remedy this problem. Such a cute-sounding name! And indeed, cookies are dainty little things—small pieces of text that can be stored by a browser and read by a server. Now that you can be identified by your cookie, a website can remember who you are, and what you've already put in your shopping basket. Unfortunately, cookies can also be used to track you from site to site, allowing advertising networks to build up a profile of your browsing habits.

Thanks to cookies, web servers can now identify and recall who you are. But how does a web browser remember that it has previously asked for a particular item from a web server? Caching!

The word *cache* always makes me think of pirates in *Treasure Island* talking about their secret caches of treasure. On the web, *caches* are also used to hoard precious items. Instead of storing doubloons and emeralds, we can use a cache to store files that we can dig up later.

Thinking about it like that, a "cache" is actually a pretty accurate term for the technology. It's certainly sounds better than "booty."

THE HTTP CACHE

Suppose you've written a web page. In that page, you've included an image. As the browser parses your page, it sees that it needs to fetch an image, and off it goes to the server. Now suppose you include that same image again later in the same page. Instead of starting another request to the server, the browser realizes that it already has a copy of that image and reuses it (**FIG 4.1**).

That's an example of the memory cache in action. It's useful for avoiding duplicate server requests, but it only works for short-term interactions. Like a goldfish, the browser for-

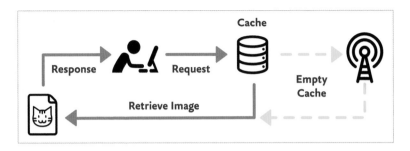

FIG 4.1: The browser can reuse images stored in the HTTP cache without sending the request out to the server.

gets about everything in its memory cache once the user leaves the page.

The browser has a longer-lasting store called the *HTTP cache* (or disk cache). If a file is stored in the HTTP cache, it can be retrieved and reused days, weeks, months, or even years later.

That sounds great, but you don't actually want all your files to be stored in the HTTP cache. If a file is updated frequently— say, the homepage of your website—it would be disastrous if it were stored in the HTTP cache. Your site's visitors would be served a stale version of the homepage.

The HTTP cache is really handy for files that are rarely, if ever, updated: images, fonts, stylesheets, and scripts. But you don't want the HTTP cache to store web pages.

To avoid storing the wrong files, the HTTP cache only does what it's told. It's up to the web server to declare which kinds of files should be cached, and for how long. This is done through the exchange of HTTP headers—the secret, behind-the-scenes instructions that accompany every response. For instance, your web server can send `max-age` headers to tell the HTTP cache how long it should store certain files. The server tells the browser that it can store images, stylesheets, and scripts for months, but that HTML pages should never be stored.

Ah, but what if you update a stylesheet or script on the server? The browser is going to do what it has been told and reuse the old version from the HTTP cache. A visitor to your site will get stale CSS or JavaScript. The visitor can overcome this by performing a hard refresh (holding down Shift while reloading the page). But putting this burden on the visitor isn't a great long-term strategy.

You could use `max-age` headers to instruct the browser to never store CSS or JavaScript files, but then you would miss out on the benefits of the HTTP cache. It would be a shame to force your site's visitors to download the same CSS and JavaScript every single time they request a page.

The most common way of breaking this impasse is to change the names of the files themselves. Suppose someone visits one of your pages, and that page links to a stylesheet called `styles-v1.css`. Using headers, you can instruct the browser to cache that file for months. When you need to change the CSS, change the name of the file to something like `styles-v2.css`. As far as the browser is concerned, this is a brand-new file that bears no relation to the CSS file stored in the HTTP cache. The browser fetches the new file and then stores it in the HTTP cache for months.

The only downside to this approach is that you also have to update every HTML page that points to the CSS or JavaScript file that you're changing the name of. On dynamic sites, there's usually a build process in place to automate this.

The HTTP cache can really boost your site's performance on repeat visits. It's a fairly crude tool though, and you can't entirely rely on it. Web browsers perform periodic clean-up operations, discarding files from the HTTP cache. There's just one HTTP cache being shared by every single website that the browser visits. There's only so much space to spare.

Now there's a successor to the HTTP cache. Using the new *Cache API*, you have much more fine-grained control over the caching of your site's content.

THE CACHE API

The Cache API is conceptually similar to the Fetch API. They are both APIs that give us access to the low-level features used by the browsers themselves. Browsers having been fetching and caching for decades, but now we can use those same mechanisms for our own purposes.

Like the Fetch API, the Cache API is asynchronous and uses promises to fulfill or reject each operation. That means you can use this API in your service worker script. You'll be able to create caches, delete caches, put files into caches, and retrieve files from caches.

Don't think of the Cache API as a replacement for the HTTP cache. Think of it as an enhancement. Don't change whatever strategy you're currently using for caching and versioning files. You can use the Cache API to create a powerful frontline caching strategy, but you will still want to keep the home fires burning with the HTTP cache.

Whereas the HTTP cache gives you one big cache for everything, the Cache API allows you to create separate caches. You could have one cache just for images, for example, and another cache for storing pages. Keeping your files in different caches gives you more control over how you treat those files.

Your first cache

Let's start with a single cache for static assets—CSS, JavaScript, fonts, icons. These are all resources that are updated infrequently.

Open up your `serviceworker.js` file. At the top of the file, choose a name for your cache and store the name in a variable like this:

```
const staticCacheName = 'staticfiles';
```

I'm using `const` for this because the value of the variable shouldn't be changed. Feel free to use a good old-fashioned `var` statement if you prefer. I've chosen to call this cache `staticfiles` and assigned that name to the variable `staticCacheName`. You can give your cache any name you like. You could call it `JohnnyCache`. Please don't.

Now that you've got a name for your cache, you'll want to create the cache and put files into it. But you'll only want to do this once, when the service worker is first installed. You can listen out for an event called `install`.

```
addEventListener('install', installEvent => {
  // Install-handling code goes here
});
```

This looks similar to how you're listening for fetch events:

```
addEventListener('fetch', fetchEvent => {
  // Fetch-handling code goes here
});
```

The difference is that the fetch event is triggered every single time the browser requests a resource, whereas the install event is only triggered when the service worker is first downloaded. You can tell the browser to delay the installation of the service worker until you've populated your cache. You're saying, "When you're about to install, wait until you've added these files to the static cache." Translating that into JavaScript, you literally say waitUntil:

```
addEventListener('install', installEvent => {
  installEvent.waitUntil(
    // Cache your files here
  ); // end waitUntil
}); // end addEventListener
```

This is the moment to use the Cache API. You'll start by using the open method of the caches object. This is a promise, so the structure looks like this:

```
caches.open(staticCacheName)
.then( cache => {
  // Success!
})
.catch( error => {
  // Failure!
});
```

There's not much we can do about errors in this case, so we won't even need to use the catch clause.

Put the `caches.open` method inside your install-handling code like this:

```
addEventListener('install', installEvent => {
  installEvent.waitUntil(
    caches.open(staticCacheName)
    .then( staticCache => {
      // Cache your files here
    }) // end open then
  ); // end waitUntil
}); // end addEventListener
```

Now you have a reference—called `staticCache`—to the open cache. This has a method called `addAll`. You can pass an array of URLs into this method:

```
staticCache.addAll(array);
```

An array is a collection of items, separated with commas, and bookended with square brackets, like this:

```
[1,2,3,4]
```

That's an array of four numbers, but you could also have an array of strings:

```
['John','Paul','George','Ringo']
```

For the `addAll` method, you're going to pass in an array of strings. Each string is the URL of a file you want to cache.

```
staticCache.addAll([
  '/path/to/stylesheet.css',
  '/path/to/javascript.js',
  '/path/to/font.woff',
  '/path/to/icon.svg'
]);
```

Those URLs are fictitious. Any resemblance to actual URLs, living or dead, is purely coincidental. Make sure that you use real URLs. If just one item in the array is misspelt, none of the URLs will be cached.

Putting it all together, you will return the result of staticCache.addAll to the install event that's patiently waiting with installEvent.waitUntil:

```
addEventListener('install', installEvent => {
  installEvent.waitUntil(
    caches.open(staticCacheName)
    .then( staticCache => {
      return staticCache.addAll([
        '/path/to/stylesheet.css',
        '/path/to/javascript.js',
        '/path/to/font.woff',
        '/path/to/icon.svg'
      ]); // end return addAll
    }) // end open then
  ); // end waitUntil
}); // end addEventListener
```

By using that return statement, you're making sure that the installation won't be completed until all the items in the array have been cached. If there are lots of files, there's a chance they won't all get cached, and then the service worker won't be installed.

To avoid that problem, you can split your list of files into the ones you *must* have and the ones you'd *like* to have. Put the must-haves behind the return statement. Put the nice-to-haves in a regular addAll:

```
addEventListener('install', installEvent => {
  installEvent.waitUntil(
    caches.open(staticCacheName)
    .then( staticCache => {
      // Nice to have
      staticCache.addAll([
        '/path/to/font.woff',
```

```
      '/path/to/icon.svg'
    ]); // end addAll
    // Must have
    return staticCache.addAll([
      '/path/to/stylesheet.css',
      '/path/to/javascript.js'
    ]); // end return addAll
  }) // end open then
); // end waitUntil
}); // end addEventListener
```

Cache, then network

Now that you've successfully made a cache filled with your static assets, you can update your service worker script to take advantage of your cache. Here's the logic of the code you'll be writing:

1) When the browser requests a file,
    a) look for a matching file that has been cached;
    b) if there's no match, fetch the file from the network.

It's time to revisit your code for handling fetch events. This is the code that will run every single time the browser requests a file from your site.

```
addEventListener('fetch', fetchEvent => {
  const request = fetchEvent.request;
  fetchEvent.respondWith(
    // fetch-handling code goes here
  ); // end respondWith
}); // end addEventListener
```

That takes care of the first part: "When the browser requests a file."

Now for the next part: "look for a matching file that has been cached." The long way of doing this is to use the open method of the caches object to specify which cache you want to search, and then use the match method to do the searching:

```
caches.open(staticCacheName)
.then( staticCache => {
  return staticCache.match(request);
});
```

The short way is to use the match method directly on the caches object. You don't need to specify which cache you want to look in:

```
caches.match(request);
```

As with all things cache-related, this is an asynchronous operation, so caches.match has the familiar structure of a promise:

```
caches.match(request)
.then( responseFromCache => {
  // Success!
})
.catch( error => {
  // Failure!
});
```

This seems straightforward enough. If we get a response from the cache, the promise is fulfilled and we can return that response. If we don't get a response, then we can instead make a fetch request for the file within the catch clause, right?

Alas, no. If match doesn't find a match for the file, the promise doesn't reject. Instead, it returns a value of null in the then clause. This makes the catch clause as useful as a window washer on a submarine.

I have no idea why match has been designed to work this way. It's like working with an annoyingly pedantic stickler.

"Hey!" you say to the Cache API. "Were you successful when you looked for this file?"

"Why, yes!" says the Cache API.

"Great!" you say. "Give it to me." Whereupon the Cache API mimes handing something to you, because it has successfully found nothing.

When you've finished rolling your eyes, you'll need to add an extra step to make sure the response isn't empty:

```
caches.match(request)
.then( responseFromCache => {
  if (responseFromCache) {
    // Success!
  }
})
```

When you write if (responseFromCache), that's shorthand for if (responseFromCache !== null). Translated to English: "Is it not empty?"

Here's how it looks inside your code:

```
addEventListener('fetch', fetchEvent => {
  const request = fetchEvent.request;
  fetchEvent.respondWith(
    caches.match(request)
    .then( responseFromCache => {
      if (responseFromCache) {
        return responseFromCache;
      } // end if
    }) // end match then
  ); // end respondWith
}); // end addEventListener
```

Notice how the return statement is used to pass the response up the chain from within caches.match to respondWith. The end result is that, if there's a matching file in the cache, the fetch event responds with the contents of that file.

That takes care of the first two parts of the flow you've outlined:

1) When the browser requests a file,
   a) look for a matching file that has been cached.

Now it's time to add the third and final part:

b) if there's no match, fetch the file from the network.

Here's the code for that:

```
return fetch(request)
.then( responseFromFetch => {
  return responseFromFetch;
});
```

In fact, you could shorten this code. Everything inside the then clause is telling the service worker to do what it would do anyway: return the response from fetching. So you can leave that part out, and the end result is the same:

```
return fetch(request);
```

If you want, you can put this in an else clause after the if statement:

```
if (responseFromCache) {
  return responseFromCache;
} else {
  return fetch(request);
}
```

In this case, the else wrapper isn't necessary. Because the if block has a return statement within it, your fetch code can go right after the if block.

```
if (responseFromCache) {
  return responseFromCache;
}
return fetch(request);
```

If you wanted to make your code even shorter, you could ditch the if statement entirely and use a single return statement:

```
return responseFromCache || fetch(request);
```

The two vertical lines mean "or," so you're saying, "Return the response from the cache, or return the result of fetching the file." The code after || will only be executed if the value before || is empty.

While that's nice and short, I'm not sure it's more understandable. Personally, I err on the side of trying to keep my code readable, even if that means the script is longer.

Putting it all together, you get something like this:

```
// When the browser requests a file...
addEventListener('fetch', fetchEvent => {
  const request = fetchEvent.request;
  fetchEvent.respondWith(
    // First, look in the cache
    caches.match(request)
    .then( responseFromCache => {
      if (responseFromCache) {
        return responseFromCache;
      } // end if
      // Otherwise fetch from the network
      return fetch(request);
    }) // end match then
  ); // end respondWith
}); // end addEventListener
```

UPDATING CACHES

You've just made big performance improvements to your site. Anyone who visits your site more than once will have a speedy experience. Static assets are coming straight out of a cache, which means the browser doesn't spend nearly as much time making network requests.

This all works wonderfully until you make a change to your CSS, or JavaScript, or some other static asset that you've put in your cache. The browser will never see the updated version. The updated file is sitting on your server, but in your service worker script, you're instructing the browser to never look on the server for that file.

The solution is similar to what we do to update the HTTP cache: throw some versioning into the mix.

You might be tempted to change the file name of your service worker script and update your HTML to point to the new script. Don't do that. Yes, a new service worker will be installed, but your old service worker will also still be installed. That's a messy state of affairs.

Instead, you want to replace the outdated service worker with a new version. To do that, you'll take care of versioning within the service worker script itself.

Your service worker script currently starts with the name of your static cache:

```
const staticCacheName = 'staticfiles';
```

Right before that, create a variable with a version number, something like this:

```
const version = 'V0.01';
```

It doesn't really matter what you name this variable, or even what value you give it, as long as you can update the value whenever you want to update the cache. You could use the current date and time as your versioning variable, if you prefer. Whatever you choose, you can then add this versioning variable to your cache name:

```
const version = 'V0.01';
const staticCacheName = version + 'staticfiles';
```

If you change your CSS or JavaScript or anything else in your cache, edit the first line of your service worker script:

```
const version = 'V0.02';
```

Because you've made a change to your service worker script—even a small change like that—the install event will be triggered again when the browser checks to see if the service worker script has been updated.

Fresh files

Wait a minute…the service worker script is written in JavaScript. Your server is probably serving JavaScript files with a long cache lifetime. After all, you want most JavaScript files to be cached. The service worker file is an exception—you want the browser to check for a new version every time.

If you have access to your server's configuration, it's a good idea to add an exception for your service worker file. If you're running an Apache server, you could add this to your .htaccess file:

```
<IfModule mod_expires.c>
  <FilesMatch "serviceworker.js">
    ExpiresDefault "access plus 0 seconds"
  </FilesMatch>
</IfModule>
```

If you don't have access to your server's configuration, not to worry. Browsers make an exception for service worker scripts. Even if your server is telling the browser to cache all JavaScript files for weeks, months, or years, a service worker script will only be cached for a maximum of twenty-four hours. So even if you can't explicitly change your server settings, the longest anyone will wait to get the updated version is one day.

If your server is set up to serve CSS and JavaScript with long cache lifetimes—as it should be—it's not enough to only update the name of your static cache in your service worker script. While that will trigger the install event, it doesn't mean that the files will be fetched directly from the server. The browser will fetch the files just as it normally does, which means it will check the HTTP cache first before going out to the network. Whatever strategy you're currently using to break out of the HTTP cache, it still applies.

If you're adding version numbers to your CSS and JavaScript file names, you'll need to update the names of those files in your service worker script too:

```
return staticCache.addAll([
```

```
  '/path/to/stylesheet-v2.css',
  '/path/to/javascript-v3.js'
]);
```

skipWaiting

Remember the service worker life cycle that we looked at in Chapter 3?

1. Download
2. Install
3. **Wait**
4. Activate

We can bypass that third step using the `skipWaiting` command in Chrome's Developer Tools. Every time you make a change to your service worker script, you can click on that `skipWaiting` link to make sure your new service worker takes control immediately, without having to close your browser window.

You can bypass this waiting phase in your code, too, by telling the service worker to take control as soon as it is installed. Use the aptly named `skipWaiting` to do this:

```
addEventListener('install', installEvent => {
  skipWaiting();
  installEvent.waitUntil(
    // Cache your files here
  ); // end waitUntil
}); // end addEventListener
```

The new service worker will take control as soon as it has been installed. The old service worker fades away into nothingness. You have removed the "waiting" step from the service worker life cycle.

When you're testing on `localhost` and making lots of changes to your service worker script, there's another very useful checkbox in Chrome's Developer Tools: Update on

Reload activates your updated service worker whenever you refresh the page.

But remember, not all refreshes are created equal. If you do a hard refresh (holding down the Shift key while you're refreshing the page), then the browser will bypass the service worker completely.

DELETING CACHES

Now you've got a way to trigger updates to your service worker—you change the version number at the top of your file:

```
const version = 'V0.03';
```

That will create a whole new cache called V0.03staticfiles:

```
const staticCacheName = version + 'staticfiles';
```

But the old caches don't go away (FIG 4.2).

The browser doesn't know that it's never going to use those caches, so it's up to you to take the garbage out. The moment that a service worker goes from installation to activation is the perfect time to take care of this—think of it as tidying up when you move into a new place. Best of all, there's an event that fires at the moment of activation. You can use that event to trigger your clean-up:

```
addEventListener('activate', activateEvent => {
  activateEvent.waitUntil(
    // Clean all the things!
  ); // end waitUntil
}); // end addEventListener
```

I'm not going to lie—the code you need to write is going to get quite complex. Don't worry if it doesn't all make sense at first.

You can access the names of all your caches using the keys method of the caches object. It is—you guessed it—a promise:

FIG 4.2: You can see all the caches in Chrome's Developer Tools under "Cache" in the sidebar of the Application panel.

```
caches.keys()
.then( cacheNames => {
  // Loop through the cacheNames array
})
```

At this point, you need to loop through the values in the cacheNames array. But you can't use a loop like you would in regular JavaScript code—that would be a synchronous operation. In service worker land, everything needs to be asynchronous, which means everything needs to be a promise. That's okay—you can create your own promise and return its result (either a fulfillment or a rejection):

```
caches.keys()
.then( cacheNames => {
  return Promise.all(
    // Asynchronous code goes here
  );
})
```

Using Promise.all allows you to wrap up a number of asynchronous operations in one return statement. All of the promises within must be fulfilled.

You've got an array called `cacheNames` that contains the names of all the caches. In the past, if I were going to loop through an array like this, I'd use something like a `for` loop. But in ES6, we've got a method called `map`, which is perfect for this situation. The `map` method is attached to the array. You can filter out the unwanted caches from the `cacheNames` array:

```
cacheNames.map( cacheName => {
  if (cacheName != staticCacheName) {
    // This cacheName needs to go!
  }
});
```

The `if` statement will find any caches with names that don't match the current static cache—notice the exclamation point that turns the question into a negative.

You can then delete each of those caches using the `delete` method of the `caches` object:

```
if (cacheName != staticCacheName) {
  return caches.delete(cacheName);
}
```

You're using a `return` statement because all of this is happening inside a promise. The `return` statement allows the promise to be fulfilled.

There's one extra step you can take once all the old caches have been deleted. Normally when a service worker becomes active, it doesn't take immediate control over any opened tabs. Instead, it waits for the user to either go to a new page or refresh the current page. That's very well-mannered of the service worker; but if you don't want it to be so deferential, you can instruct it to take control immediately.

The command for this is `clients.claim`. You can put this instruction in another `then` clause after you've dealt with old caches. With asynchronous events, chaining `then` clauses together is how you ensure that your code executes in the order you want.

In this case, there's nothing to pass into the then clause, so there's a pair of parentheses before the arrow instead. It looks like the worst emoticon ever:

```
.then( () => {
  return clients.claim();
})
```

Putting it all together, your activation code looks like this:

```
addEventListener('activate', activateEvent => {
  activateEvent.waitUntil(
    caches.keys()
    .then( cacheNames => {
      return Promise.all(
        cacheNames.map( cacheName => {
          if (cacheName != staticCacheName) {
            return caches.delete(cacheName);
          } // end if
        }) // end map
      ); // end return Promise.all
    }) // end keys then
    .then( () => {
      return clients.claim();
    }) // end then
  ); // end waitUntil
}); // end addEventListener
```

That looks quite complex. Don't worry if you don't understand all of it. To be honest, I don't understand it myself. Please don't tell anyone.

The truth is that your activation code and your installation code will remain largely unchanged from project to project. You can copy and paste code with only minor changes. If you don't understand the code completely, that's okay.

In short, use the install event to cache some files; use the activate event to delete old caches.

```
addEventListener('install', installEvent => {
```

```
  // Cache some files
});
addEventListener('activate', activateEvent => {
  // Delete old caches
});
```

But the code you write for the fetch event...well, that's a different story. That code can be as unique as your website. That's where the magic happens.

5 SERVICE WORKER STRATEGIES

YOU'VE MADE SOME GREAT performance enhancements to your website. Using the combined power of the Cache API and the Fetch API, you're making your site nice and zippy.

If you recall, here's the logic of your `fetch` events:

1) When the browser requests a file,
   a) look for a matching file that has been cached;
   b) if there's no match, fetch the file from the network.

You can go further. You can add another step:

c) If the file can't be fetched, show a fallback instead.

There are a few reasons why a file couldn't be fetched. Perhaps your server has been taken down for maintenance, or perhaps the user has lost their internet connection. The end result is the same—the file that the user is requesting is unavailable.

At the close of Chapter 3, you saw how you could create a fallback response to deal with this situation:

```
return new Response(
  '<h1>Oops!</h1> <p>Something went wrong.</p>',
  {
    headers: {'Content-type': 'text/html;
  charset=utf-8'}
  }
);
```

Now that you've mastered the power of caching, you can create a much richer fallback. You can make a fallback page ahead of time—then, when the user requests a page that's unavailable, you can channel your inner TV chef and declare, "Here's one I made earlier!"

YOUR OFFLINE PAGE

Start by creating your fallback page. I usually put this at the root of the site, so it has a URL like /offline.html. In this page, you can make use of any of the assets—styles, scripts, fonts, and images—that you are putting in your static cache.

Once you've got your offline page up and running, add its URL to the list of files in your static cache. Update the list of files in the code you've written for the install event:

```
const version = 'V0.04';
const staticCacheName = version + 'staticfiles';
addEventListener('install', installEvent => {
  installEvent.waitUntil(
    caches.open(staticCacheName)
    .then( staticCache => {
      // These files don't block installation
      staticCache.addAll([
        '/path/to/font.woff',
        '/path/to/icon.svg'
      ]); // end addAll
      // These files must be cached for installation
      return staticCache.addAll([
        '/path/to/stylesheet.css',
```

```
            '/path/to/javascript.js',
            '/offline.html'
        ]); // end return addAll
    }) // end open then
  ); // end waitUntil
}); // end addEventListener
```

Your code for the `activate` event remains the same as before—you still want to clean up old caches before activating the updated service worker.

But the code you've written for every `fetch` event needs to be updated. The part where you attempt to fetch from the network currently doesn't have a `then` clause or a `catch` clause:

```
return fetch(request);
```

A `catch` clause would be the perfect place to, well, "catch" any problems:

```
return fetch(request)
.catch( error => {
  // Serve up a fallback
});
```

In this case, your fallback is the offline page that you've put in your cache:

```
return fetch(request)
.catch( error => {
  return caches.match('/offline.html');
});
```

There's that familiar pattern of passing results up the chain using `return` statements. At one end of the chain is `fetchEvent.respondWith`. At the other end of the chain is the `catch` clause. If that `catch` code is executed, the offline page is the response that's sent back.

Putting it all together, your fetch-handling code looks like this:

```
addEventListener('fetch', fetchEvent => {
  const request = fetchEvent.request;
  fetchEvent.respondWith(
    // First look in the cache
    caches.match(request)
    .then( responseFromCache => {
      if (responseFromCache) {
        return responseFromCache;
      } // end if
      // Otherwise fetch from the network
      return fetch(request)
      .catch( error => {
        // Show a fallback page instead
        return caches.match('/offline.html');
      }); // end fetch catch and return
    }) // end match then
  ); // end respondWith
}); // end addEventListener
```

You can test how well this is working by going offline. Just as we learned in Chapter 3, the simplest solution is to tick the checkbox marked Offline in Chrome's Developer Tools. (Remember to make sure that the latest version of your service worker is installed and activated first). Now if you refresh the page, you'll be rewarded with your glorious custom offline page.

Notice that the URL doesn't change—you aren't redirected to /offline.html. Rather, the content of that fallback page is served up as a temporary replacement for the usual content of the page you're trying to access.

Much like an oh-so-clever 404 page, your offline page is another opportunity to show off your brand. Instead of showing your site's visitors a generic offline dinosaur, you can regale them with a witty message of sympathy (assuming that's in your brand's wheelhouse) (FIG 5.1).

Hotel comparison website Trivago has a particularly nice fallback: if a page is unavailable, you can try completing a maze instead (FIG 5.2).

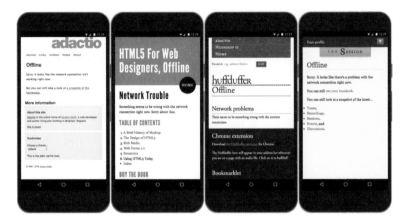

FIG 5.1: A selection of custom offline pages.

FIG 5.2: Trivago's offline maze game.

CHOOSING YOUR STRATEGY

Your fetch-handling code can be tweaked to accommodate all kinds of circumstances. A service worker script written for one site might not be a good fit for a different site—the `install` and `activate` code may require only minor tweaking, but the `fetch` code should be designed on a case-by-case basis.

Sniffing headers

There are plenty of sites where the text content is updated frequently, but images are unlikely to change. In that situation, you might want to write different logic for HTML requests and image requests. You can do that by looking in the headers of the request. The `Accept` header will tell you what kind of file is being requested:

```
request.headers.get('Accept')
```

You have access to `request.headers`, which is an array. The `get` method allows you to find the exact header you want, which in this case is the `Accept` header.

The `includes` method is perfect for searching one string for a shorter string. You can ask if the `Accept` header includes the string `text/html`:

```
request.headers.get('Accept').includes('text/html')
```

This will give a true or false answer. That makes it perfect for an `if` statement. An `if` statement expects a true/false question for it to evaluate:

```
if (request.headers.get('Accept').includes('text/
  html')) {
  // True!
} else {
  // False!
}
```

Repeating this pattern allows you to build up a logical structure to your fetch-handling code:

```
addEventListener('fetch', fetchEvent => {
  const request = fetchEvent.request;
  if (request.headers.get('Accept').includes('text/
  html')) {
    // HTML-handling logic goes here
  } else if (request.headers.get('Accept').
  includes('image')) {
    // Image-handling logic goes here
  } else {
    // Logic for everything else goes here
  }
});
```

If you don't like all of the if/else pairing going on, you could flatten the structure a bit by using return statements inside each if block. That way, if the code inside the if block is executed, none of the code after that will be executed:

```
addEventListener('fetch', fetchEvent => {
  const request = fetchEvent.request;
  if (request.headers.get('Accept').includes('text/
  html')) {
    // HTML-handling logic goes here
    return; // Go no further
  }
  if (request.headers.get('Accept').
  includes('image')) {
    // Image-handling logic goes here
    return; // Go no further
  }
  // Logic for everything else goes here
});
```

A strategy for pages

For HTML files, you probably want to serve up the freshest possible version. Your logic might look something like this:

1) When the user requests an HTML file,
   a) fetch that page from the network;
   b) otherwise show the fallback page.

Here's how that translates into code:

```
// When the user requests an HTML file
if (request.headers.get('Accept').includes('text/
  html')) {
  fetchEvent.respondWith(
    // Fetch that page from the network
    fetch(request)
    .catch( error => {
      // Otherwise show the fallback page
      return caches.match('/offline.html');
    }) // end fetch catch
  ); // end respondWith
  return; // Go no further
} // end if
```

A strategy for images

You could also have a whole other cache—separate from your existing cache for static files—that's just for storing images. This will make repeat visits speedier and speedier, loading images straight from the cache for repeat visitors. The logic would look like this:

1) Every time a visitor makes a request for an image,
   a) look for a cached version of the image;
   b) otherwise fetch the image from the network
      i) and put the image in the cache.

First of all, you'll need to name your new cache—let's call it images—alongside your existing cache for static files. There's no need to add versioning to this one.

```
const version = 'V0.04';
const staticCacheName = version + 'staticfiles';
const imageCacheName = 'images';
```

Near the start of your service worker script, create an array that contains the names of your caches. You could call it cache-List:

```
const cacheList = [
  staticCacheName,
  imageCacheName
];
```

You'll need to update the filtering part of your activation code. Currently it's looking to see whether the name of the cache being checked isn't equal to the name of the static cache:

```
if (cacheName != staticCacheName) {
  return caches.delete(cacheName);
}
```

Change that line of code so that it's now looking to see whether there's a matching name in your cacheList array. The includes method is perfect for this:

```
if (!cacheList.includes(cacheName)) {
  return caches.delete(cacheName);
}
```

See that exclamation mark? The if statement is asking if the cacheList array does *not* include cacheName.
Your updated activation code looks like this:

```
addEventListener('activate', activateEvent => {
  activateEvent.waitUntil(
```

```
caches.keys()
.then( cacheNames => {
  return Promise.all(
    cacheNames.map( cacheName => {
      if (!cacheList.includes(cacheName)) {
        return caches.delete(cacheName);
      } // end if
    }) // end map
  ); // end return Promise.all
}) // end keys then
.then( () => {
  return clients.claim();
}) // end then
); // end waitUntil
}); // end addEventListener
```

Now for the fetch-handling code. Here's the logic again:

1) When the user requests an image,
   a) look for a cached version of the image;
   b) otherwise fetch the image from the network
      i) and put the image in the cache.

Here's the first part in code:

```
// When the user requests an image
if (request.headers.get('Accept').includes('image'))
  {
  fetchEvent.respondWith(
```

For the second step, it doesn't matter which cache the image is in. It might be in the static cache, or it might be in the cache dedicated to images. In that situation, you can use the catch-all caches.match instead of opening a specific cache by name:

```
// Look for a cached version of the image
caches.match(request)
.then( responseFromCache => {
  if (responseFromCache) {
```

```
  return responseFromCache;
}
```

If there's no match found in any cache, you'll need to move on to the next step—fetching the image:

```
// Otherwise fetch the image from the network
return fetch(request);
```

Here it is in its expanded form:

```
// Otherwise fetch the image from the network
return fetch(request)
.then( responseFromFetch => {
  return responseFromFetch;
});
```

It's worth remembering that "fetch" doesn't strictly mean "Fetch this from the network." It means, "Do what you would do anyway." The browser will first look in the HTTP cache before making a network request.

Either way, once you have the image, you don't want to just serve it up. There's one other step before that: put the image in the cache.

You can use the put method to add a file to a cache. You give it the name of the file, and the contents. But if you try putting the contents of responseFromFetch directly into a cache, you'll run into problems:

```
// Otherwise fetch the image from the network
return fetch(request)
.then( responseFromFetch => {
  // Put the image in the cache
  caches.open(imageCacheName)
  .then( imageCache => {
    // This will cause an error!
    imageCache.put(request, responseFromFetch);
  });
  return responseFromFetch;
});
```

It turns out that you can only use responseFromFetch once. That's because responseFromFetch isn't a standalone chunk of data like a string or an object. It's a stream of data. Once that data has been streamed, it can't be used again.

That's okay. You can make a copy of the data using the clone method, then you can put the copy into the cache while you're returning the original response:

```
// Otherwise fetch the image from the network
return fetch(request)
.then( responseFromFetch => {
  // Put a copy in the cache
  const copy = responseFromFetch.clone();
  caches.open(imageCacheName)
  .then( imageCache => {
    imageCache.put(request, copy);
  });
  return responseFromFetch;
});
```

There's a little bit of a problem here. You're hoping that the copy will be put into the cache at the same time as you're sending the response back to the browser. There's a chance that the service worker might "power down" once the user has received the response. If that happens, the copy might never end up in the cache.

It's not the end of the world if that happens—the important thing is that the browser sends the user a response. Still, you can make sure that the copy gets cached by invoking waitUntil on the fetchEvent. You're telling the fetchEvent to stay active until the caching code completes, even if a response has already been received:

```
// Otherwise fetch the image from the network
return fetch(request)
.then( responseFromFetch => {
  // Put a copy in the cache
  const copy = responseFromFetch.clone();
  fetchEvent.waitUntil(
```

```
      caches.open(imageCacheName)
      .then( imageCache => {
        return imageCache.put(request, copy);
      })
    );
    return responseFromFetch;
  });
```

Here's all the code for your image-handling logic:

```
// When the user requests an image
if (request.headers.get('Accept').includes('image'))
  {
  fetchEvent.respondWith(
    // Look for a cached version of the image
    caches.match(request)
    .then( responseFromCache => {
      if (responseFromCache) {
        return responseFromCache;
      } // end if
      // Otherwise fetch the image from the network
      return fetch(request)
      .then( responseFromFetch => {
        // Put a copy in the cache
        const copy = responseFromFetch.clone();
        fetchEvent.waitUntil(
          caches.open(imageCacheName)
          .then( imageCache => {
            return imageCache.put(request, copy);
          }) // end open then
        ); // end waitUntil
        return responseFromFetch;
      }); // end fetch then and return
    }) // end match then
  ); // end respondWith
  return; // Go no further
} // end if
```

A strategy for everything else

That still leaves other types of files, like CSS and JavaScript. The logic for handling those files could be:

1) For everything else,
   a) look for a cached copy of the file;
   b) otherwise fetch the file from the network.

Here's that logic translated into code:

```
// For everything else...
fetchEvent.respondWith(
  // Look for a cached copy of the file
  caches.match(request)
  .then( responseFromCache => {
    if (responseFromCache) {
      return responseFromCache;
    } // end if
    // Otherwise fetch the file from the network
    return fetch(request);
  }) // end match then
); // end respondWith
```

Putting it all together

Now you've got different code for different kinds of files:

1. The code for handling HTML pages (try the network first, otherwise show a fallback)
2. The code for handing images (try the cache first, otherwise go to the network and keep a copy)
3. The code for handling everything else (try the cache first, otherwise go to the network)

Here's your logic in English:

1) When the user requests an HTML file,
   a) fetch that page from the network;

b) otherwise show the fallback page.
2) When the user requests an image,
    a) look for a cached version of the image;
    b) otherwise fetch the image from the network
        i) and put a copy in the cache.
3) For everything else,
    a) look for a cached version of the file;
    b) otherwise fetch from the network.

Translating all of that into code, you get this:

```
addEventListener('fetch', fetchEvent => {
  const request = fetchEvent.request;
  // When the user requests an HTML file
  if (request.headers.get('Accept').includes('text/
html')) {
    fetchEvent.respondWith(
      // Fetch that page from the network
      fetch(request)
      .catch( error => {
        // Otherwise show the fallback page
        return caches.match('/offline.html');
      }) // end fetch catch
    ); // end respondWith
    return; // Go no further
  } // end if
  // When the user requests an image
  if (request.headers.get('Accept').
includes('image')) {
    fetchEvent.respondWith(
      // Look for a cached version of the image
      caches.match(request)
      .then( responseFromCache => {
        if (responseFromCache) {
          return responseFromCache;
        } // end if
        // Otherwise fetch the image from the
network
        return fetch(request)
```

```
      .then( responseFromFetch => {
        // Put a copy in the cache
        const copy = responseFromFetch.clone();
        fetchEvent.waitUntil(
          caches.open(imageCacheName)
          .then( imageCache => {
            return imageCache.put(request, copy);
          }) // end open then
        ); // end waitUntil
        return responseFromFetch;
      }); // end fetch then and return
    }) // end match then
  ); // end respondWith
  return; // Go no further
} // end if
// For everything else...
fetchEvent.respondWith(
  // Look for a cached version of the file
  caches.match(request)
  .then( responseFromCache => {
    if (responseFromCache) {
      return responseFromCache;
    } // end if
    // Otherwise fetch the file from the network
    return fetch(request);
  }) // end match then
); // end respondWith
}); // end addEventListener
```

Phew! It's quite overwhelming to see pages of JavaScript like that, isn't it? Bear in mind that what looks like one big block of code is made up of smaller self-contained pieces. As long as you understand what's happening within the individual parts, don't worry about how intimidating it looks when they're all joined together.

If the code doesn't work for you, don't despair. Often the problem turns out to be a single mistyped character. JavaScript is less forgiving than CSS or HTML—you need to make sure your curly braces and parentheses all match up. The JavaScript console in your browser's developer tools can help you track down where the problem might be. Most of the time it turns out to be a stray comma, a missing period, or some other punctuation problem.

I find it helps to imagine I'm in a film like *Sneakers*, *Hackers*, or *War Games*. It doesn't make debugging any easier, but I feel better about myself.

6 REFINING YOUR SERVICE WORKER

I'M SURE YOU CAN COME UP WITH some additions to your service worker script. Take a second look at the image logic, for example:

1) When the user requests an image,
    a) look for a cached version of the image;
    b) otherwise fetch the image from the network
        i) and put a copy in the cache.

That doesn't take into account the worst-case scenario: What if the image can't be retrieved from the cache or the network? Take a leaf out of the strategy you're using for HTML—you could add one final conditional step to your image-handling logic:

    c) Otherwise show a fallback image.

For this to work, you'd need to update your `install` event code. The fallback image would need to be included in your static assets, just like your offline page:

```
staticCache.addAll([
  '/path/to/stylesheet.css',
  '/path/to/javascript.js',
  '/offline.html',
  '/fallback.svg'
]);
```

Don't forget to update your version variable too:

```
const version = 'V0.05';
```

Now you can add a `catch` clause to the part of your image-handling code where you try fetching from the network:

```
.catch( error => {
  return caches.match('/fallback.svg');
})
```

Here's how your updated image-handling code looks:

```
// When the user requests an image
if (request.headers.get('Accept').includes('image'))
  {
  fetchEvent.respondWith(
    // Look for a cached version of the image
    caches.match(request)
    .then( responseFromCache => {
      if (responseFromCache) {
        return responseFromCache;
      } // end if
      // Otherwise fetch the image from the network
      return fetch(request)
      .then( responseFromFetch => {
        // Put a copy in the cache
        const copy = responseFromFetch.clone();
        fetchEvent.waitUntil(
          caches.open(imageCacheName)
          .then( imageCache => {
            return imageCache.put(request, copy);
```

```
      }) // end open then
    ); // end waitUntil
    return responseFromFetch;
  }) // end fetch then
  .catch( error => {
    // Otherwise show a fallback image
    return caches.match('/fallback.svg');
  }); // end fetch catch and return
  }) // end match then
); // end respondWith
return; // Go no further
} // end if
```

To recap, here's your updated logic for images:

1) When the user requests an image,
   a) look for a cached version of the image;
   b) otherwise fetch the image from the network
      i) and put a copy in the cache;
   c) otherwise show a fallback image.

FETCHING FRESH IMAGES

I spot another opportunity to update the logic for your images. The current logic is working great, but the image cache never gets fresh copies of images—they're only added to the cache the first time they're fetched. You could expand the logic to keep the cache updated regardless:

1) When the user requests an image,
   a) look for a cached version of the image,
      i) fetch a fresh version from the network
         (1) and update the cache;
   b) otherwise fetch the image from the network
      i) and put a copy in the cache;
   c) otherwise show a fallback image.

Here's the code where you carry out the first two steps:

```
// When the user requests an image
if (request.headers.get('Accept').includes('image'))
  {
  fetchEvent.respondWith(
    // Look for a cached version of the image
    caches.match(request)
    .then( responseFromCache => {
      if (responseFromCache) {
        return responseFromCache;
      }
```

You can update that if block to include the new extra steps:

```
if (responseFromCache) {
  // Fetch a fresh version from the network
  fetchEvent.waitUntil(
    fetch(request)
    .then (responseFromFetch => {
      // Update the cache
      caches.open(imageCacheName)
      .then( imageCache => {
        return imageCache.put(request,
  responseFromFetch);
      }); // end open then
    }) // end fetch then
  ); // end waitUntil
  return responseFromCache;
} // end if
```

Now your cache of images won't ever get too stale.

I think we've covered some good ways of optimizing our fetch-handling code for images. Now let's look at handling web pages.

CACHING WEB PAGES

The current logic for your HTML pages is fairly straightforward. There are only two possibilities: either the user gets the page they want directly from the network, or they get a fallback page:

1) When the user requests an HTML file,
   a) fetch that page from the network;
   b) otherwise show the fallback page.

But suppose you had a separate cache just for pages. Then you could introduce an intermediate step to your logic:

1) When the user requests an HTML file,
   a) fetch that page from the network;
   b) otherwise look for a cached version of the page;
   c) otherwise show the fallback page.

You'll need to make a new cache for pages. Like the images cache, this one doesn't need to be versioned:

```
const version = 'V0.05';
const staticCacheName = version + 'staticfiles';
const imageCacheName = 'images';
const pagesCacheName = 'pages';
```

Then update your list of valid cache names:

```
const cacheList = [
  staticCacheName,
  imageCacheName,
  pagesCacheName
];
```

You could prepopulate that new cache during the `install` event. But remember, that event only fires once. Any files you put in a cache at that point will remain unchanged. That's great for static files like CSS, JavaScript, and fonts, but it's not ideal for web pages that are updated frequently.

Instead, you could repeat what you're doing with images, and populate the cache as you go. Every time the user visits a page, put a copy of that page in the cache:

1) When the user requests an HTML file,
   a) fetch that page from the network
      i) and put a copy in the cache;
   b) otherwise look in the cache;
   c) otherwise show the fallback page.

You're still treating images and pages differently—for images, you look in the cache first; for pages, you try the network first. In both cases you're building up a bigger and bigger cache as the user explores your site.

The code for dealing with pages remains the same to begin with:

```
// When the user requests an HTML file
if (request.headers.get('Accept').includes('text/
  html')) {
  fetchEvent.respondWith(
    // Fetch that page from the network
    fetch(request)
```

Now you can introduce a then clause to put a copy of the response into the cache:

```
.then( responseFromFetch => {
  // Put a copy in the cache
  const copy = responseFromFetch.clone();
  fetchEvent.waitUntil(
    caches.open(pagesCacheName)
    .then( pagesCache => {
      return pagesCache.put(request, copy);
    })
  );
  return responseFromFetch;
})
```

With that code in place, your site's visitors will build up a cache of pages as they travel around your site. If they lose their network connection, you can try showing them a cached version of the page they're requesting. As long as they've visited it at least once before, the page should be in the cache.

You can use the `catch` clause to search your caches:

```
.catch( error => {
  return caches.match(request);
})
```

Finally, if all else fails, serve up the fallback page. You'll need to expand your `catch` clause to find out whether the `match` returned a meaningful response. If the response was empty, grab the fallback page from your static cache:

```
.catch( error => {
  return caches.match(request)
  .then( responseFromCache => {
    if (responseFromCache) {
      return responseFromCache;
    }
    return caches.match('/offline.html');
  });
})
```

Putting all that together, here's your updated code for handling pages:

```
// When the user requests an HTML file
if (request.headers.get('Accept').includes('text/
  html')) {
  fetchEvent.respondWith(
    // Fetch that page from the network
    fetch(request)
    .then( responseFromFetch => {
      // Put a copy in the cache
      const copy = responseFromFetch.clone();
      fetchEvent.waitUntil(
```

```
        caches.open(pagesCacheName)
        .then( pagesCache => {
          return pagesCache.put(request, copy);
        }) // end open then
      ); // end waitUntil
      return responseFromFetch;
    }) // end fetch then
    .catch( error => {
      // Otherwise look for a cached version of the
page
      return caches.match(request)
      .then( responseFromCache => {
        if (responseFromCache) {
          return responseFromCache;
        } // end if
        // Otherwise show the fallback page
        return caches.match('/offline.html');
      }); // end match then and return
    }) // end fetch catch
  ); // end respondWith
  return; // Go no further
} // end if
```

And with that, you've created a really nice offline experience. If someone is browsing your site, they might lose their internet connection and never even notice—they'll still be able to view any pages they previously visited.

HANDLING URLS

So far, your fetch-handling logic has been based on file types: HTML, images, and everything else. If you wanted, you could apply different logic depending on other factors, like which part of your site is being requested.

Here's a fairly typical example: Let's say you've got a site that publishes articles. Those articles might appear under a particular URL like /posts/ or /articles/. If the content of those articles rarely changes after publication, you might as well try serving them from the cache instead of the network. That way, the user will get a really speedy response.

You can still choose to update the cache with a fresh copy of the page. Then the next time the user visits that page, they'll get a fresher version. The version they get from the cache will be slightly out of date—it will be one version behind—but if the changes are likely to be minor corrections, the slightly stale nature of the response is a small tradeoff for the super-speedy response time.

You probably wouldn't want to serve up a cached version of your homepage, where content freshness is a priority. That's fine—you can write different code for different scenarios. Instead of only looking at the file type, you can also look at the URL being requested.

Here's how you're starting your fetch-handling code:

```
addEventListener('fetch', fetchEvent => {
  const request = fetchEvent.request;
```

That `request` object has a property called `url`. You can use this to look for specific strings of text, like `/products/` or `/articles/`:

```
if (request.url.includes('/articles/')) {
  // Logic for article pages goes here
  return;
}
```

If you need more fine-grained control in that `if` statement, you can use a regular expression with the `test` method:

```
if (/\/articles\/.+/.test(request.url)) {
  // Now you've got two problems
  return;
}
```

That's looking for the string `/articles/` followed by at least one other character...I think. Regular expressions are my kryptonite.

However you decide to do it, being able to apply different logic to different URL patterns opens up a whole world of possibilities.

Here's the logic you might apply for article pages if you want to prioritize speed over freshness:

1) When the requested page is an article,
    a) look in the cache,
        i) fetch a fresh version from the network
            (1) and update the cache;
    b) otherwise fetch the page from the network
        i) and put a copy in the cache;
    c) otherwise show the fallback page.

Here we go:

```
// When the requested page is an article
if (/\/articles\/.+/.test(request.url)) {
  fetchEvent.respondWith(
```

Start by looking for a match from the cache:

```
// Look in the cache
caches.match(request)
.then( responseFromCache => {
  if (responseFromCache) {
```

Before sending back the response from the cache, use waitUntil to fetch a fresh version in the background:

```
// Fetch a fresh version from the network
fetchEvent.waitUntil(
  fetch(request)
```

When we get a fresh copy, put it in the cache:

```
.then( responseFromFetch => {
  // Update the cache
  caches.open(pagesCacheName)
```

```
.then( pagesCache => {
  return pagesCache.put(request,
responseFromFetch);
  });
})
```

Finally, don't forget to send back the response from the cache:

```
return responseFromCache;
```

Putting those steps together, you get this:

```
// Look in the cache
caches.match(request)
.then( responseFromCache => {
  if (responseFromCache) {
    // Fetch a fresh version from the network
    fetchEvent.waitUntil(
      fetch(request)
      .then( responseFromFetch => {
        // Update the cache
        caches.open(pagesCacheName)
        .then( pagesCache => {
          return pagesCache.put(request,
responseFromFetch);
        }); // end open then
      }) // end fetch then
    }; // end waitUntil
    return responseFromCache;
  } // end if
```

The next part—"otherwise fetch the page from the network"—follows the familiar pattern:

```
// Otherwise fetch the page from the network
return fetch(request);
```

But it needs to be expanded for the additional step—"and put a copy in the cache":

```
// Otherwise fetch the page from the network
return fetch(request)
.then( responseFromFetch => {
  // Put a copy in the cache
  const copy = responseFromFetch.clone();
  fetchEvent.waitUntil(
    caches.open(pagesCacheName)
    .then( pagesCache => {
      return pagesCache.put(request, copy);
    })
  );
  return responseFromFetch;
})
```

Finally there's the last resort—"otherwise show the fall-back page":

```
// Otherwise show the fallback page
.catch( error => {
  return caches.match('/offline.html');
});
```

Putting it all together, you get this:

```
// When the requested page is an article
if (/\/articles\/.+/.test(request.url)) {
  fetchEvent.respondWith(
    // Look in the cache
    caches.match(request)
    .then( responseFromCache => {
      if (responseFromCache) {
        // Fetch a fresh version from the network
        fetchEvent.waitUntil(
          fetch(request)
          .then( responseFromFetch => {
            // Update the cache
            caches.open(pagesCacheName)
            .then( pagesCache => {
```

```
            return pagesCache.put(request,
    responseFromFetch);
          }); // end open then
        }) // end fetch then
      ); // end waitUntil
      return responseFromCache;
    } // end if
    // Otherwise fetch the page from the network
    return fetch(request)
    .then( responseFromFetch => {
      // Put a copy in the cache
      const copy = responseFromFetch.clone();
      fetchEvent.waitUntil(
        caches.open(pagesCacheName)
        .then( pagesCache => {
          return pagesCache.put(request, copy);
        }) // end open then
      ); // end waitUntil
      return responseFromFetch;
    }) // end fetch then
    .catch( error => {
      // Otherwise show the fallback page
      return caches.match('/offline.html');
    }); // end fetch catch and return
  }) // end match then
); // end respondWith
return; // Go no further
} // end if
```

That's a hefty chunk of code! You can put all of it right inside the `if` statement that checks for HTML requests:

```
// When the user requests an HTML file
if (request.headers.get('Accept').includes('text/
  html')) {
  // When the requested page is an article
  if (/\/articles\/.+/.test(request.url)) {
    // Look in the cache
      // Fetch a fresh version from the network
```

```
            // Update the cache
        // Otherwise fetch the page from the network
          // Put a copy in the cache
        // Otherwise show the fallback page
        return;
    }
    // Otherwise fetch the page from the network
      // Put a copy in the cache
    // Otherwise look in the cache
    // Otherwise show the fallback page
    return;
}
```

That gives you different priorities for different kinds of pages. For articles, try the cache first. For other pages, try the network first.

PATTERNS

Your code is getting quite long. It's daunting to have so much JavaScript. That's why I find comments in the code so helpful—they help me keep track of what's going on where.

Even though you have many lines of code, the overall structure of that code is made up of repeating patterns:

- Using if statements to test for certain conditions.
- Looking for files in caches.
- Fetching files from the network.
- Putting copies of files into a cache.

Those are the building blocks, and, just like pieces of LEGO, they can be arranged into an almost infinite variety of configurations.

The logic for article pages and images is a particularly powerful pattern. Because you're looking in the cache first before trying the network, a returning visitor to your site will get the content they want almost instantly. It doesn't matter whether they're online, offline, or on an intermittent connection—in some ways, having a flaky connection is worse than having no connection at all. That's why this pattern can make such a difference to the user experience.

Offline First

This "cache first, then network" pattern has been labelled *Offline First* (you can hear the capital letters when people say it). It's a somewhat misleading moniker. You can't offer a truly offline-first experience—the user must visit your site at least once to get the benefit. But it's useful shorthand for a way of thinking about how people might interact with your site.

This approach makes no assumptions about the kind of network connection someone might have. In much the same way that a service worker can be thought of as an enhancement to your existing site, the Offline First approach treats the network itself as an enhancement.

There are some situations where you can apply Offline First thinking to the entire site. An in-browser game that doesn't include team play could be cached in its entirety. I published a book online at resilientwebdesign.com that doesn't require an internet connection to be read. The contents of the book hardly ever change (apart from the occasional fixed typo), so caching the entire thing feels like a safe bet.

Still, it's somewhat presumptuous. After all, people don't have an infinite amount of room on their devices. So let's look at other ways to make our service workers as respectful as possible.

7

TIDYING UP

YOU MIGHT BE WONDERING how much space your service worker gets to play with. Just how many pages and images can you keep caching?

There isn't a fixed amount of space set aside for service worker caches. There are a number of browser technologies—like localStorage, IndexedDB, and the Cache API—that share the space available on a device. There's often a remarkably large amount of space to share, sometimes gigabytes of it.

Still, storage isn't limitless. When a device starts to get full, it will attempt to do some cleaning up. But even at this point, your service worker caches won't be the first to go. The HTTP cache is the first place where the browser will do some spring cleaning. That's one reason why a bespoke service worker cache is more reliable than the shared HTTP cache.

Even though the files in your caches are fairly safe, you still don't want to hoard any more than you need to. If every website started storing megabytes and megabytes of files, it would turn into a tragedy of the commons.

MANAGING SPACE

You can be a good citizen of the web by only caching files that you're pretty sure will get used. You're already doing the right thing by deleting old caches during the `activate` event. It would be nice if you could also periodically clean up individual caches by putting a cap on the number of files they can store.

Perhaps you don't need to store every single article someone has ever read on your site; the most recent twenty or thirty articles viewed might be enough. Likewise, you don't need to hold on to every image forever; limiting your image cache to fifty or sixty images might be enough.

You need some code to trim down the number of items in a specified cache. This is the perfect job for a function—a reusable chunk of code that you can run more than once. Let's call the function `trimCache` and have it accept two arguments—the name of the cache to trim, and the maximum number of items we want the cache to store:

```
function trimCache(cacheName, maxItems) {
  // Trim the number of items in cacheName to
  maxItems
```

Open up the specified cache and get a list of all the items in it using the `keys` method:

```
cacheName.open( cache => {
  cache.keys()
  .then( items => {
```

In this situation, you don't care *what* the items are—you just want to know *how many* there are. You can find out by querying the `length` property of `items`. You can compare that number to the `maxItems` argument:

```
if (items.length > maxItems)
```

If there are too many items in the cache (i.e. more than `max-Items`), you can delete an item.

You don't want to delete the freshest item in the cache. It makes more sense to delete the oldest item—the first one in the array. Whereas we humans like counting from one, computers like to start with zero. That's why the first item in an array has an index of zero, rather than one:

```
cache.delete(items[0])
```

Then you can repeat the whole operation:

```
.then(
  trimCache(cacheName, maxItems)
);
```

That will repeat the function with the same parameters. It will continue to loop until the number of items in the cache has been reduced to the value of maxItems.

Putting that all together, your function looks like this:

```
function trimCache(cacheName, maxItems) {
  cacheName.open( cache => {
    cache.keys()
    .then( items => {
      if (items.length > maxItems) {
        cache.delete(items[0])
        .then(
          trimCache(cacheName, maxItems)
        ); // end delete then
      } // end if
    }); // end keys then
  }); // end open
} // end function
```

Your function is ready and waiting to be called. But when should you call it?

You could call the function from the activate event handler—that's where you're cleaning up out-of-date caches. But that event is triggered when someone returns to your site. If someone spends a long time browsing your site—and doesn't return—their caches could get quite full. It would be better if you could trigger the `trimCache` function every time someone visits a page of your site. The `fetch` event seems like the right time to do this, but things could get messy if you're already using that event to add items to caches.

The ideal time to trigger the `trimCache` function is after a page has loaded. You can't access that event directly in your service worker script, but you can send instructions from a web page to a service worker using a method called `postMessage`.

postMessage

Most of the logic in your service worker script is attached to events: `install`, `activate`, and `fetch`. But there's one other useful event. It's called `message`:

```
addEventListener('message', messageEvent => {
  // Do something with messageEvent
});
```

This event can be triggered from any page that's currently being controlled by the service worker. You can find out if a page is being controlled by a service worker by checking for the existence of `navigator.serviceWorker.controller`. Currently, your HTML page has a bit of feature detection like this:

```
<script>
if (navigator.serviceWorker) {
  navigator.serviceWorker.register('/serviceworker.
  js');
}
</script>
```

You can add a further bit of feature detection before assuming that a service worker is up and running:

```
<script>
if (navigator.serviceWorker) {
```

```
navigator.serviceWorker.register('/serviceworker.
js');
if (navigator.serviceWorker.controller) {
  // A service worker is up and running!
}
}
</script>
```

Now you can safely trigger a message event from inside that if statement. Use the `postMessage` method of `navigator.serviceWorker.controller`:

```
navigator.serviceWorker.controller.postMessage(...);
```

You can put anything you like inside the argument for post-Message. You could, for example, send a string of text like "clean up caches":

```
<script>
if (navigator.serviceWorker) {
  navigator.serviceWorker.register('/serviceworker.
  js');
  if (navigator.serviceWorker.controller) {
    window.addEventListener('load', function () {
      navigator.serviceWorker.controller.
    postMessage('clean up caches');
    });
  }
}
</script>
```

The message "clean up caches" is sent once the page has finished loading. That message is now accessible from your service worker script through the message event. It shows up as a property of the event called data:

```
addEventListener('message', messageEvent => {
  console.log(messageEvent.data);
});
```

If you add that code to your service worker script, when your page loads you'll see this message in the console of your browser's developer tools:

```
clean up caches
```

Now, instead of logging the message to the console, use it to trigger the `trimCache` function you wrote:

```
addEventListener('message', messageEvent => {
  if (messageEvent.data == 'clean up caches') {
    trimCache(pagesCacheName, 20);
    trimCache(imageCacheName, 50);
  }
});
```

That will trim the cache of pages down to twenty items, and the cache of images down to fifty. I chose those numbers at random; use whatever amounts are right for your site. Whatever you choose, the important thing is that you're practicing good cache hygiene. The Cache API gives you a lot of power. Now you're wielding that power in a responsible way.

FUNCTIONS

Your `trimCache` function is a perfect example of abstracting code into a reusable chunk. Whenever you find yourself writing the same kind of code more than once, it might be a good idea to turn that chunk of code into a function so that you can reuse it.

The fetch-handling code in your service worker script probably has some duplicated functionality scattered throughout. An example would be wherever your logic includes this flow:

1) Fetch a file from the network,
   a) open a cache
      i) and put the file into the cache.

You could wrap that logic up into a reusable function called stashInCache. The details will change each time you need to use this code—Which file to fetch? Which cache to put it in? Turn those details into arguments. Call them, say, request and cacheName:

```
function stashInCache(request, cacheName) {
  // Fetch the file
  fetch(request)
  .then( responseFromFetch => {
    // Open the cache
    caches.open(cacheName)
    .then( theCache => {
      // Put the file into the cache
      return theCache.put(request,
responseFromFetch);
    }); // end open then
  }); // end fetch then
}
```

Here's an example of where you might use this stashIn-Cache function. In your logic for images, you have a step where you fetch and then cache a fresh version of the image:

1) When the user requests an image,
   a) look for a cached version of the image;
      i) fetch a fresh version from the network
       (1) and update the cache.

Now you can replace those last two steps with a call to the stashInCache function:

```
// When the user requests an image
if (request.headers.get('Accept').
includes('image')) {
  fetchEvent.respondWith(
    // Look for a cached version of the image
    caches.match(request)
    .then( responseFromCache => {
```

```
      if (responseFromCache) {
        // Fetch and cache a fresh version
        fetchEvent.waitUntil(
          return stashInCache(request,
imageCacheName);
        ); // end waitUntil
        return responseFromCache;
      } // end if
```

There's also this logic for handling article pages:

1) When the requested page is an article,
   a) look in the cache;
      i) fetch a fresh version from the network
         (1) and update the cache.

Here's the code for that, but this time it's using the stash-InCache function:

```
// When the requested page is an article
  if (/\/articles\/(.+)/.test(request.url)) {
    fetchEvent.respondWith(
      // Look in the cache
      caches.match(request)
      .then( responseFromCache => {
        if (responseFromCache) {
          // Fetch and cache a fresh version
          fetchEvent.waitUntil(
            return stashInCache(request,
pagesCacheName);
          ); // end waitUntil
          return responseFromCache;
        } // end if
```

Now you've managed to avoid some code duplication. As an added bonus, you've also managed to reduce the amount of nesting in your fetch-handling code. I find that the more deeply nested my code gets, the harder it is to read.

Coding style

Because promises are asynchronous, whenever you want to do something with the result of a promise, you have to do so inside a then clause. If the logic you're trying to code is "Do this, and then do that, and then do something else", you'll find your code is nested three levels deep.

The stashInCache function is a typical example of this. There are three steps—"fetch the file, open the cache, and put the file into the cache"—but each step depends on the result of the step before. That's why the structure of the code looks like an arrowhead—each step in the process depends on the step before.

```
function stashInCache(request, cacheName) {
  // Fetch the file
  fetch(request)
  .then( responseFromFetch => {
    // Open the cache
    caches.open(cacheName)
    .then( theCache => {
      // Put the file into the cache
      return theCache.put(request,
  responseFromFetch);
    }); // end open then
  }); // end fetch then
} // end function
```

If you tried to rewrite the function without the nested then clauses, your code wouldn't work:

```
function stashInCache(request, cacheName) {
  // Fetch the file
  const responseFromFetch = fetch(request);
  // Open the cache
  const theCache = caches.open(cacheName);
  // Put the file into the cache
  return theCache.put(request, responseFromFetch);
}
```

The browser will execute that return statement before there's a final value for responseFromFetch or theCache (because both fetch and caches.open are asynchronous). That's a shame. The sequential code looks so much nicer than the nested code.

Async functions

Now there's a way to write code that *looks* sequential, but actually waits for each promise to resolve!

If you use the magic word async when you declare your function, then you can use the word await within that function.

```
async function stashInCache(request, cacheName) {
  // Fetch the file
  const responseFromFetch = await fetch(request);
  // Open the cache
  const theCache = await caches.open(cacheName);
  // Put the file into the cache
  return await theCache.put(request,
  responseFromFetch);
}
```

That function looks like a series of three sequential statements, so it's nice and easy to read. But because of the await keyword, you can go ahead and reference responseFromFetch and theCache in your closing statement. The async function is sending back a promise. That promise won't be resolved until responseFromFetch and theCache have values (when both fetch and caches.open have been resolved).

The upshot of all this is that async functions allow you to rewrite your code to look neater. Async functions don't provide any new functionality; they're just another way to write code that deals with promises. Your service worker script is filled with code that handles promises, so if you wanted to, you could rewrite your code completely.

Rewriting promises

Here's an example of a straightforward promise, written the old-fashioned way. It's responding to a fetch event by retrieving the request from the network:

```
fetchEvent.respondWith(
  fetch(request)
); // end respondWith
```

Here's the same functionality rewritten as an anonymous async function:

```
fetchEvent.respondWith(
  async function() {
    return await fetch(request);
  }() // end async function
); // end respondWith
```

The extra pair of parentheses at the close of the async function are there so that the function is executed straightaway. Those parentheses are necessary for the code to work, but I wish they weren't—the end of the code looks like somebody tried to encode some very complex emotions into a text message.

So far, the async function isn't making the code any clearer. Here's a slightly more complex logic example:

1) Try fetching the file from the network;
2) otherwise look for a cached version of the file.

Here's the code for that, using fetch and catch:

```
fetchEvent.respondWith(
  // Try fetching the file from the network
  fetch(request)
  .catch( error => {
    // Otherwise look for a cached version of the
    file
```

```
    return caches.match(request)
  }) // end fetch catch
); // end respondWith
```

To rewrite that functionality using `async` and `await`, you'll need to rephrase your logic using `try` and `catch`:

```
fetchEvent.respondWith(
  async function() {
    try {
      // Try fetching the file from the network
      return await fetch(request);
    } // end try
    catch (error) {
      // Otherwise look for a cached version of the
  file
      return await caches.match(request);
    } // end catch
  }() // end async function
); // end respondWith
```

Everything inside the curly braces after `try` is your first choice. Everything inside the curly braces after `catch` will only be executed if your first choice doesn't work out (notice that there isn't a dot before the word `catch` this time).

Apart from the extra parentheses at the end, that code reads quite nicely. I also like the politeness of using a `try` statement, as though you're gently saying to the service worker: "Hey there, buddy, give it your best shot. And if it doesn't work out, well, I'll be there to catch you. Literally...with a `catch` statement."

Finally, here's a three-step process:

1) Try fetching the file from the network;
2) otherwise look for a cached version of the file;
3) otherwise show the fallback page.

That's a typical service worker strategy for HTML pages. Here's the code:

```
fetchEvent.respondWith(
  // Try fetching the file from the network
  fetch(request)
  .catch( error => {
    // Otherwise look for a cached version of the
file
    return caches.match(request)
    .then( responseFromCache => {
      if (responseFromCache) {
        return responseFromCache;
      } // end if
      // Otherwise show the fallback page
      return caches.match('/offline.html');
    }); // end match then and return
  }) // end fetch catch
); // end respondWith
```

Here's the same functionality, rewritten as an `async` function:

```
fetchEvent.respondWith(
  async function() {
    try {
      // Try fetching the file from the network
      return await fetch(request);
    } // end try
    catch (error) {
      // Otherwise look for a cached version of the
file
      const responseFromCache = await caches.
match(request);
      if (responseFromCache) {
        return responseFromCache;
      } // end if
      // Otherwise show the fallback page
      return caches.match('/offline.html');
    } // end catch
  }() // end async function
); // end respondWith
```

If you find the async functions easier to read, then consider updating your code. But if you're happy with the old-school style of promises, you can leave your code be. It's your decision—use whatever coding style makes the most sense to you.

Remember that the style of your code doesn't change its functionality. When it comes to the functionality of your service worker, you've got all the building blocks you need to program just about anything you can imagine.

It's time to leave the service worker script and look at a different file that you can make improvements to—your offline page.

8 THE OFFLINE USER EXPERIENCE

WE HAVEN'T REALLY TALKED about the contents of /offline.
html, the fallback page you made for the situation when all else
fails. It's entirely up to you what you put on that page—something silly or something useful. If you decide to make it useful,
the Cache API can help.

So far, you've used the power of the Cache API from within
your service worker script. But the Cache API can be accessed
from other places too. You can call forth the power of the Cache
API from your web pages, including your offline page.

You've got a cache of pages that your site's visitor has accu-
mulated on their journey through your site. If that visitor loses
their internet connection, they may end up looking at your fallback page. Wouldn't it be nice if you could show them a list of
pages that they can visit even without an internet connection?

You can put this list together by looping through the items
in your cache of pages:

1) Open the cache of pages;
2) loop through each item in the cache
    a) and make a link to the URL of each page;
3) finally, display the list of links.

This code can go inside /offline.html:

```
<p>You can still read these pages:</p>
<ul id="history"></ul>
<script>
// Open the cache of pages
caches.open('pages')
.then( pagesCache => {
  pagesCache.keys()
  .then(keys => {
    let markup = '';
    // Loop through each item in the cache
    keys.forEach( request => {
      // Make a link to the URL of each page
      markup += `<li><a href="${request.
  url}">${request.url}</a></li>`
;
    });
    // Display the list of links
    document.getElementById('history').innerHTML =
  markup;
  }); // end keys then
}); // end open
</script>
```

That's not bad. Now visitors to your site have something to do while they're offline (**FIG 8.1**).

This could be better though. For a start, we're only displaying pages that the user has previously visited. It might be nice if the user could explicitly mark which pages they want to save for offline reading. You could provide the functionality of Instapaper or Pocket, right from your own site.

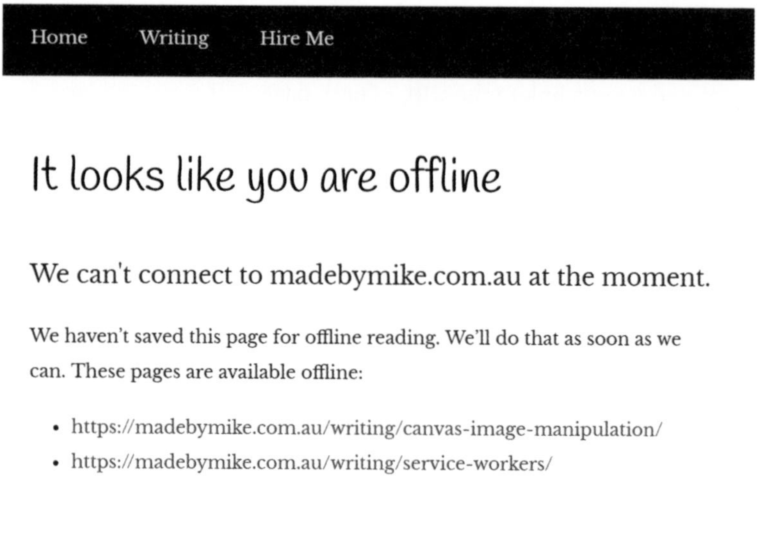

Home   Writing   Hire Me

It looks like you are offline

We can't connect to madebymike.com.au at the moment.

We haven't saved this page for offline reading. We'll do that as soon as we can. These pages are available offline:

- https://madebymike.com.au/writing/canvas-image-manipulation/
- https://madebymike.com.au/writing/service-workers/

FIG 8.1: Mike Riethmuller's offline page shows which articles are available to read offline (http://bkaprt.com/go/08-01/).

SAVE FOR OFFLINE

A visitor to your site needs some mechanism to save a page for offline reading. I think a button is the right element to use for this—an accessible, all-purpose trigger for handling user interaction—but a checkbox could work too:

```
<button class="btn--offline">save for offline</
    button>
```

You can use CSS to make the button look however you want. You could put the button directly in the HTML of your page, but seeing as it's only going to work for browsers that support service workers, I think it's better to inject the button into the page using JavaScript. You can put the JavaScript inside a script element at the end of each page, or you could put it in an external file that you link to from a `script` element at the end of each page.

Use some feature detection so that only browsers that support service workers will get the button. Here's the logic:

1) If this browser supports service workers,
   a) create a button element,
   b) and add the button to the page.

And here's the code for that logic:

```
// If this browser supports service workers
if (navigator.serviceWorker) {
  // Create a button element
  const offlinebutton = document.
  createElement('button');
  offlinebutton.innerText = 'save for offline';
  offlinebutton.className = 'btn--offline';
  // Add the button to the page
  document.body.appendChild(offlinebutton);
}
```

That will add the button to the end of the page, but you might want to put it somewhere more convenient, or use CSS to position it.

Clicking that button will do absolutely nothing. Let's change that. Inside your feature-detecting `if` statement, you can add an event listener to the button:

```
offlinebutton.addEventListener('click', function
  (event) {
  // Save for later
});
```

(I'm regressing to old-fashioned JavaScript without arrow functions. I'm a lot warier of using newer syntax outside the safe confines of a service worker script.)

The first thing to do is avoid the button-press triggering a page submission:

```
offlinebutton.addEventListener('click', function
  (event) {
    event.preventDefault();
```

You can also store a handy reference to the button that has just been clicked:

```
const offlinebutton = this;
```

At this point it might be a good idea to give some feedback to the user. Let them know that something is happening. You could update the text inside the button:

```
offlinebutton.innerText = 'saving...';
```

It's time to crack open the Cache API. You can use an entirely new cache for this. Let's call it "savedpages":

```
caches.open('savedpages')
```

Use the add method to fetch and cache the contents of the current page. You'll need to pass in the URL of the current page, which you can get from window.location.href:

```
caches.open('savedpages')
.then( function (cache) {
  cache.add(window.location.href)
})
```

When the page has been cached, you might want to give some feedback to the user. You could update the text inside the button again:

```
caches.open('savedpages')
.then( function (cache) {
  cache.add(window.location.href)
  .then( function () {
    offlinebutton.innerText = 'saved for offline!';
  }); // end add then
}); // end open then
```

Here's how the event-handling code looks now:

```
// When the button is pressed...
offlinebutton.addEventListener('click', function
  (event) {
  event.preventDefault();
  const offlinebutton = this;
  // Provide some feedback to the user
  offlinebutton.innerText = 'saving...';
  // Open a cache
  caches.open('savedpages')
  .then( function (cache) {
    // Add the URL of the current page to the cache
    cache.add(window.location.href)
    .then( function () {
      // Provide some feedback to the user
      offlinebutton.innerText = 'saved for
offline!';
    }); // end add then
  }); // end open then
}); // end addEventListener
```

You have successfully cached the page at the user's request.

The functionality of your offline page—which currently shows a list of URLs—is fine, but it could be better. Wouldn't it be nice if it could also show the title of the page? And maybe a description too? That's why this is a good opportunity to store metadata about the page you're caching.

The Cache API can't help you here. You need to reach for another API instead.

localStorage

Browsers have many APIs for storing data. The IndexedDB API is quite powerful, and it's asynchronous, which is always good. Alas, it's also quite complex and tricky to get to grips with.

There's a much simpler API called localStorage. It isn't asynchronous, so you shouldn't use it for anything too intensive, but it is pleasantly straightforward.

It has two methods: setItem and getItem. They do exactly what you'd expect them to do.

You can pass two arguments into the setItem method—a key and a value:

```
localStorage.setItem('name', 'Jeremy Keith');
```

The getItem method takes one argument—pass in a key, and it will return the corresponding value:

```
const myname = localStorage.getItem('name');
```

You can use the setItem method to store metadata when the user is saving a page to read later. Then, on your offline page, you can use the getItem method to retrieve that information.

There's a nifty trick that allows you to store lots of data in a single localStorage value: JSON.

JSON stands for JavaScript Object Notation. Technically, JSON is JavaScript. There are no functions or loops. There are only variables, written in key/value pairs like this:

```
const data = {
  "key": "value",
  "other_key": "another value"
}
```

Those curly braces create a new JavaScript object. Each key is a property of the object (remember, a property is nothing more than a variable which happens to be scoped within an object). You can then access those values using dot notation like data.key or data.other_key.

First, create a JSON object with all the data you want to store. Then use `JSON.stringify` to put it all into `localStorage`. If you use the URL of the current page as the key, you can associate as much information as you want with it.

```
const data = {};
localStorage.setItem(
  window.location.href,
  JSON.stringify(data)
);
```

So, if you want to store the title of the current page, you could grab that from the `title` element like this:

```
const data = {
  "title": document.querySelector('title').innerText
};
```

Or you might want to grab the text from the first `h1` element on the page. It's up to you.

If you have a `meta` element with a description of the page, you could store the contents of that too:

```
const data = {
  "title": document.querySelector('title').
  innerText,
  "description": document.
  querySelector('meta[name="description"]').
  getAttribute('content')
};
```

You can store as much or as little information as you want. Think about what you might want to display on your offline page. For instance, if there's a publication date somewhere on the page, you might want to store that information.

Whatever you decide, you can update your caching code to store this metadata:

```
caches.open('savedpages')
.then( function (cache) {
  cache.add(window.location.href)
  .then( function () {
    const data = {
      "title": document.querySelector('title').
    innerText,
      "description": document.
    querySelector('meta[name="description"]').
    getAttribute('content')
      };
    localStorage.setItem(
      window.location.href,
      JSON.stringify(data)
    );
    offlinebutton.innerText = 'saved for offline!';
  }); // end add then
}); // end open then
```

Now you've got a one-to-one mapping between the saved-pages cache and localStorage, both of which are using URLs as keys. If there's a URL in the savedpages cache, then there's a corresponding chunk of metadata accessible through that URL with localStorage.getItem.

You can rewrite the JavaScript in /offline.html to take advantage of the data in localStorage. Here's the updated logic for that:

1) Open the cache of saved pages;
2) loop through each item in the cache;
   a) **look up the corresponding metadata in local storage**
   b) and make a descriptive link to the URL of each page;
3) finally, display the list of links.

That translates into something like this:

```
<p>You can still read these pages:</p>
<div id="history"></div>
<script>
let markup = '';
// Open the cache of saved pages
caches.open('savedpages')
.then( pagesCache => {
  pagesCache.keys()
  .then(keys => {
    // Loop through each item in the cache
    keys.forEach( request => {
      // Look up the corresponding metadata in local
    storage
      const data = JSON.parse(localStorage.
    getItem(request.url));
      // Make a descriptive link to the URL of each
    page
      if (data) {
        markup += `<h3><a href="${request.
    url}">${data.title}</a></h3>`
;
        markup += `<p>${data.description}</p>`
;
      }
    });
    // Finally, display the list of links
    document.getElementById('history').innerHTML =
    markup;
  }); // end keys then
}); // end open then
</script>
```

It's similar to what you had before, but the metadata saved in localStorage allows you to present the user with a more readable list of pages to read (FIG 8.2). Best of all, these are all pages that the user has chosen to save offline, so you're no longer guessing what they might want.

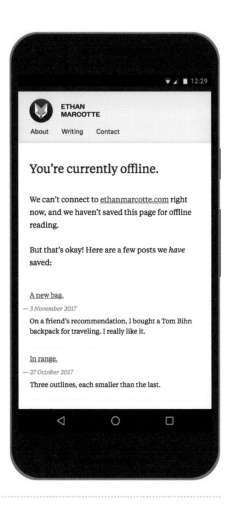

FIG 8.2: The offline page on Ethan Marcotte's site shows metadata for every article you can read offline (http://bkaprt.com/go/08-02/).

INCREMENTAL IMPROVEMENTS

Now you're providing a good offline experience—but, as with any web experience, there's always room for improvement.

For instance, when someone saves a page for offline reading, you could cache any images used in that page. You could create a separate cache for those images like, say, `savedimages`. At the moment the user clicks the button to save a page, you'll need to execute this logic:

1) Find all the `img` elements in the current page (hint: the DOM method `querySelectorAll` is your friend);
2) loop through all of those images
   a) and get the URL for each one (hint: it's the value of the `src` attribute);
3) put all of those images in the `savedimages` cache (hint: the `addAll` method of the Cache API accepts an array of URLs).

If your site uses lots of videos or audio files, you might want to cache those too. The logic would be very similar.

There's also room for improvement in how you present the Save for Offline button to your site's visitors. What if someone is looking at a page that they've previously saved? The button still reads "Save for Offline." It would be nice if you could present a different option in that situation—perhaps you don't want to show the button at all. Or perhaps the button could say "Saved for Offline," and clicking it would remove the page from the cache. You would need to add some extra steps at the point where you inject the button into the page. You could, for example, check to see if there's an entry for the current page in localStorage.

Once you start looking at ways to improve the user experience, there's almost no limit to what you can accomplish. There are all kinds of powerful browser APIs to investigate. APIs like Background Sync and Notifications allow service workers to execute actions even when the browser isn't open. Data can be synced and your site's visitors can receive notifications even when their phones are in their pockets!

That sounds a lot like what native apps can do, doesn't it? That's no accident. Slowly but surely, web browsers are allowing the kind of functionality that previously only native apps could provide. There's even a name for websites that take full advantage of modern browser features. They're called *progressive web apps*.

9 PROGRESSIVE WEB APPS

WHEN WEB DESIGNER FRANCES BERRIMAN coined the term progressive web app in 2015, she said: "The name is for your boss, for your investor, for your marketeer." In other words, we say it because it sounds cool ().

And those three little words pack a powerful punch:

- **Progressive.** This word echoes the philosophy of *progressive enhancement,* the idea that websites should be built in a layered way: make sure that the core functionality is available to the most amount of people, with extra functionality added on for more capable browsers and devices. In my experience, it's the most sensible way to build anything for the web, including progressive web apps—which makes sense when you consider how a service worker can only take effect once someone has already started interacting with your site.
- **Web.** As in, not native. For a long time, if you wanted to build something that worked offline, a native app was your only option. Now, you can build an offline-capable product on the web and publish it instantly, without going through the approval process of any app store. There's so much that

can be done in web browsers these days (thanks, service workers!) that it's hard to justify the expense of creating separate native apps for every platform.

- **App.** This is probably the least accurate word in the whole phrase. After all, what is an "app" anyway? We all know examples of apps, but I have yet to hear a good definition. And as we've seen, service workers can be applied to just about any website, whether it's an app or not. Progressive web apps don't really have anything to do with apps, but, as Berriman said: "It's marketing, just like HTML5 had very little to do with actual HTML."

Marketing is not to be sniffed at when it comes to web technologies. For instance, back in 2004, web developers started using techniques to update parts of a page instead of refreshing the whole page—but it became much easier to talk about it once Jesse James Garrett coined the term *Ajax* to describe it.

Similarly, in 2010, when developers were struggling to make desktop websites work on mobile devices, Ethan Marcotte introduced the phrase *responsive web design*—and sparked a whole movement.

Of course, responsive web design wasn't just a cool-sounding phrase. The technique had a clear definition that was made up of three parts: fluid grids, fluid images, and media queries. Likewise, the term *progressive web app* doesn't just sound good in a meeting—it *also* has a clear definition, made up of three parts. For a website to qualify as a progressive web app, it must:

1. be served over HTTPS,
2. work offline with a service worker, and
3. have a Web App Manifest file.

The good news is that you've already checked off two of the three actions in that to-do list. The even better news is that the third item is by far the easiest to achieve.

WEB APP MANIFEST

To start, create a blank file called `manifest.json`. I recommend storing it at the root level of your site (/manifest.json), just as you've done with your service worker script (/serviceworker.js).

This file will contain metadata: data about data. Historically, we've filled the head of HTML documents with metadata. But at some point, it started to get out of hand. There were lines of metadata specifically for Apple devices, more lines of metadata specifically for Android devices, and even more lines of metadata specifically for Windows devices.

To bring things back under control, we got the Web App Manifest. Its purpose is twofold. First, it standardizes the metadata, regardless of device manufacturer. Second, instead of repeating all that metadata in every HTML file, the metadata resides in one place.

Instead of filling the head of your HTML documents with lines and lines of metadata, you now only need one line: a `link` element with a `rel` value of `"manifest"` and an `href` value pointing to your file:

```
<link rel="manifest" href="/manifest.json">
```

Now web browsers know where to look for your manifest file.

A Web App Manifest has absolutely nothing to do with an AppCache manifest. I just wanted to make that clear, in case you've previously attempted to use AppCache (and if so, you have my sympathies). A Web App Manifest is a JSON file.

You've already written some JSON for your `localStorage` script. The JSON has curly braces on the outside and key/value pairs inside them:

```
{
  "key": "value",
  "other_key": "another value"
}
```

So a JSON file is actually a file containing a single JavaScript object. All of the key/value pairs are properties of the object. The property names (keys) of a Web App Manifest are being standardized by the World Wide Web Consortium (W3C):

> This specification defines a JSON-based manifest file that pro-
> vides developers with a centralized place to put metadata
> associated with a web application. This metadata includes, but
> is not limited to, the web application's name, links to icons, as
> well as the preferred URL to open when a user launches the
> web application. (http://bkaprt.com/go/09-02/)

Time to fill up this JSON file with metadata.

lang

Start by declaring the language of your website. If your site is in English, here's how you declare that in your manifest file:

```
"lang": "en"
```

name

The name property is pretty straightforward—it's the name of your website:

```
"name": "My Website"
```

short_name

The full name of your website might be a bit too long to fit in some spaces. Think about the space taken up by an application's icon on a phone screen. Anything more than twelve characters runs the risk of being truncated. The short_name property allows you to specify the shortened alias of your site:

```
"short_name": "Website"
```

description

The `description` property can be used to provide a sentence or two describing what your website does:

```
"description": "This is my website. There are many
   like it but this one is mine."
```

theme_color

The `theme_color` property is nifty. You provide a color value that browsers can use to "fill in" their interface. Visitors to your site get a browser window customized to your site's color scheme (**FIG 9.1**).

If your site has a solid color across the top, or uses a background color, that color value is a good candidate for this property. Give the value in the same way that you would declare a color in CSS. Here's an example of a hexadecimal value for a nice shade of blue:

```
"theme_color": "#336699"
```

You can also provide this in a `meta` element in the `head` of your HTML documents if you like:

```
<meta name="theme-color" content="#336699">
```

background_color

The `background_color` property is similar to the `theme_color` property. A lot of the time, you can supply the same value for both properties. But think of the `background_color` property as the loading screen for your site (**FIG 9.2**). Choose a color to fill the screen that matches the branding of your site:

```
"background_color": "#336699"
```

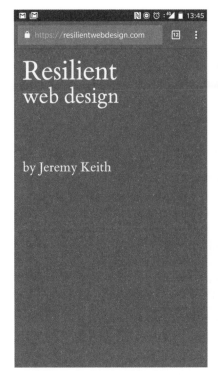

FIG 9.1: The interface of the Chrome browser on Android takes on the `theme_color` specified in the Web App Manifest for the web book *Resilient Web Design* (http://bkaprt. com/go/09-03/).

FIG 9.2: The Session is a progressive web app with a mustard-flavored `background_color` value (http://bkaprt. com/go/09-04/).

start_url

If someone were to bookmark your site, which URL would you like them to start from? For most sites, this will be the homepage, but you have the option of specifying any page using the `start_url` property:

```
"start_url": "/"
```

display

If someone has bookmarked your website, then (on some mobile devices) this property determines how your site will launch when the bookmark is activated:

```
"display": "standalone"
```

The display property accepts one of four values: browser, minimal-ui, standalone, or fullscreen:

- A display value of browser will launch your site as normal. It will appear in a browser tab, complete with address bar.
- A display value of minimal-ui will launch your site with much less browser interface on display.
- If you specify a display value of standalone or fullscreen, then your site will start up as though it were a native app (**FIG 9.3**). There won't be any address bar, or indeed any indication that it's a website.

With the fullscreen option, even the operating system's task bar will be covered up. That could be useful if you're building a game that needs to take over the whole screen.

Having your website behave exactly like a native app sounds appealing, but please take the time to stop and think about what your users might end up missing out on. If your site launches in standalone or fullscreen mode, how will visitors be able to share individual URLs? Normally they could copy the URL in the address bar, but if you banish the address bar, then you'll have to provide that functionality yourself. And, without the browser's usual interface, visitors to your site will have no back or forward options. You will need to make sure that your navigation accounts for that.

So, while the standalone and fullscreen options sound good, there are many times when the browser or mimimal-ui value is the right one for your progressive web app.

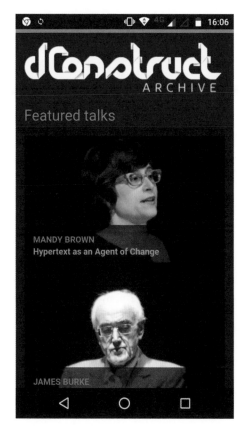

FIG 9.3: The dConstruct archive is a progressive web app that launches with a `display` value of `standalone` (http://bkaprt.com/go/09-05/).

icons

Up until now, every property in your JSON file has had one value—a string of text. The `icons` property can accept multiple values. To do that, you can use an array:

```
"icons": []
```

Then each item in the array can be a whole new object. In the case of the `icons` array, each item within it can have its own `src`, `sizes`, and `type` properties:

```
"icons": [
  {
    "src": "/images/small-icon.png",
    "sizes": "48x48",
    "type": "image/png"
  },
  {
    "src": "/images/large-icon.jpg",
    "sizes": "512x512",
    "type": "image/jpeg"
  }
]
```

You can provide as many icons as you want. The images should be square. It's a good idea to make sure there's a fairly large one in there—at least 512 pixels square. You can use whatever image formats you like: JPG, PNG, or SVG. When someone bookmarks your website, the browser can then choose the most appropriate image to associate with your site. Quite often, manifest files will feature the same image—usually a logo—at many different sizes. You could make the larger-sized versions more detailed, and keep the smaller ones simpler.

Putting all of that metadata together, our Web App Manifest code looks like this:

```
{
  "lang": "en",
  "name": "My Website",
  "short_name": "Website",
  "description": "This is my website. There are many
  like it but this one is mine.",
  "theme_color": "#336699",
  "background_color": "#336699",
  "start_url": "/",
  "display": "standalone",
  "icons": [
    {
      "src": "/images/small-icon.png",
      "sizes": "48x48",
```

```
      "type": "image/png"
    },
    {
      "src": "/images/large-icon.jpg",
      "sizes": "512x512",
      "type": "image/jpeg"
    }
  ]
}
```

With the introduction of nested curly braces for icons, your JSON is getting a bit more complex. The order of the properties doesn't matter, and many of them are optional—but make sure your commas are all in the right place. Whenever I've got a problem with my JSON, it's usually either a missing comma, or a comma where there shouldn't be one. You can test your JSON by copying and pasting it into the form at .

HOMESCREEN

Browsers have always offered the option to bookmark websites so that you can get back to them quickly. On mobile devices, there's another option: You can save a website to the homescreen of the device, where its icon sits alongside the icons of native apps.

Usually a visitor to your site has to actively seek out the Add to Homescreen option from their browser's interface. But Google's Chrome for Android can actually prompt visitors to your progressive web app to add it to their homescreen (**FIG 9.4**).

In order for this prompt to appear, these conditions need to be met:

- The site must be running on HTTPS.
- The site must have a service worker that will display something when the user is offline.
- The site must have a Web App Manifest file.
- The manifest must have a name value and a short_name value.

- The manifest must have an icon that's at least 144 pixels square.
- The user must visit the site more than once in a relatively short space of time.
- The manifest must have a `display` value of `minimal-ui`, `standalone` or `fullscreen`.

If your site fulfills those conditions, then visitors using Chrome on Android will be prompted to add it to their homescreen.

This is wonderful! By introducing this algorithm, Google found a way to promote progressive web apps. If a website fulfills all the criteria for the prompt to appear, then the user can be confident that it's a site worth bookmarking. As a site owner, you get rewarded for following best practices. Everybody wins.

If you use a `display` property of `standalone` or `fullscreen`, then once your website's been added to the homescreen, it will be treated exactly like a native app (**FIG 9.5**). It will appear in the app switcher, just like a native app. From the user's point of view, there's no distinction. And with features like notifications now possible through the web, there's no reason for the user to prefer a native app over a well-made progressive web app.

BE PROGRESSIVE

The early days of the responsive web weren't smooth sailing. Developers tried to make mobile-friendly sites by adding a sprinkling of media queries, but they were still starting from a desktop-first mindset. That led to frustration and disappointment. It took time for people to realize that a mobile-first approach made more sense. Even then, there was a tendency for designers and developers to focus on the specific dimensions of the latest and greatest mobile devices instead of letting the content dictate the breakpoints.

But we got there eventually. Over time, it became normal for websites to adapt to mobile devices, tablets, and desktop displays. Users came to expect that responsive behavior.

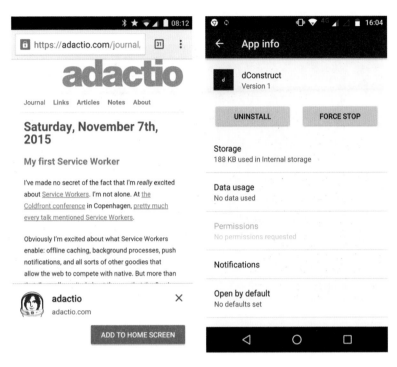

FIG 9.4: Chrome on Android prompting a visitor to my site to add it to their homescreen (adactio.com).

FIG 9.5: A progressive web app that has been added to the homescreen is treated the same as a native app.

Device-specific URLs—such as m-dot subdomains—became ever rarer.

Progressive web apps have also been through an awkward early childhood. Many of the initial examples were made to only work on mobile devices, despite the fact that the "progressive" part of progressive web apps means they should work for everyone, regardless of device or browser (**FIG 9.6**).

Creating progressive web apps in silos, separate from the "real" website, feels like a step backwards to the days before responsive web design. As a minimum baseline, progressive web apps should be responsive.

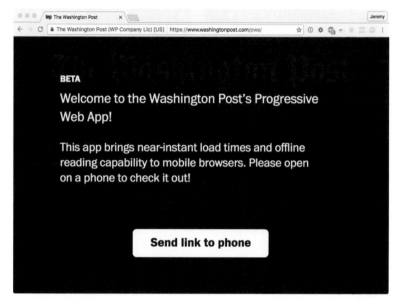

FIG 9.6: The Washington Post's first progressive web app turned away perfectly capable desktop browsers.

There's also been a tendency for developers to go a bit overboard with the "app" part of *progressive web app*. Many of the early progressive web apps were entirely JavaScript-driven and tried to closely mimic the behaviors of native apps. This led to a widespread misunderstanding that progressive web apps had to be client-side, single-page apps built from scratch. But as you've seen in this book, just about any existing website can be turned into a progressive web app by:

- running the site on HTTPs,
- adding a service worker script, and
- creating a Web App Manifest file.

That's it.

Planning your progressive web app

If you're building a progressive web app from scratch, I recommend taking a layered approach.

1. Start with the content. What's the fundamental action that someone needs to be able to do on your site? For some sites, it's reading. For others, it's shopping. For yet others, it's sharing photos or videos.
2. Once you've identified the core functionality, think about the simplest technology to make it work. Not the best. The simplest. Quite often, the answer is good ol' HTML sent from a web server, where all the smart logic resides.
3. When you've built that, then you can start to layer on more and more functionality. Use the latest and greatest CSS. Take advantage of all the wonderful JavaScript APIs available in modern browsers. If some browsers don't support those features, that's okay; you've made sure that they can still accomplish the core task.

It's during that third phase that you can go wild with service workers. You can make sure that returning visitors to your site will have a fast, reliable experience.

We can learn a lot by looking to native apps. If there are design patterns or interactions that work well, we can apply them to our progressive web apps. But we should be careful not to simply imitate native apps wholesale. There's one feature of the web that native apps can't match: URLs.

The power of URLs

Instead of making your users go to an app store, find your app, and then install it (assuming they have the bandwidth to do that), you can give them the URL of your website. You can give them the URL in an email, or on another site, or written on a poster. Once they visit your site—just once—they've got what they need. What an amazing way of distributing software!

If someone keeps returning to your site, maybe they'll add it to their homescreen. That's like installing a native app, but with one big difference: there's nothing more to install. Putting your site's icon on the homescreen is merely a convenient shortcut. There's no hefty download. Everything's already cached.

That process is also great for developers. Without app stores, there's no need to go through an approval process to publish a progressive web app. And whenever you need to make a change to the site, you don't need to submit an update for approval—you simply make the change.

Native apps rely on app stores for distribution. Progressive web apps use URLs. The World Wide Web becomes one big app store, but an app store where everyone is free to publish without asking for permission.

URLs are the standout feature of the web. We should learn what we can from the design of native apps, but let's not lose sight of what makes the web great. I think it's wonderful that we can create sites that provide an amazing, rich experience in the latest browsers, but still work perfectly well for older or less capable devices.

THE FUTURE

We live in paradoxical times. Web technology has never been more powerful. We can create incredible layouts with CSS; we can deploy lightweight optimized images; we can access device sensors through JavaScript APIs; we can even go offline using service workers.

Yet, for many people, using the web is painful. Despite all the wonderful advances in web technology, too many websites are bloated, buggy, and slow. No wonder people think that native apps are somehow inherently better—a typical web experience can be an exhausting trial, especially on mobile.

Sturgeon's Law states that 90% of everything is crud. Alas, that certainly seems to hold true when browsing the web on a mobile device. You could see this as an opportunity to differentiate yourself from the competition. If 90% of websites are too big and slow, your nimble performant site should stand out from the herd.

But the truth is that we all suffer if the web is perceived to be unusable. We need to work to change that perception. It will be a challenge, but I think we can do it. Progressive web apps can light the way to a brighter future.

My friend Remy Sharp described the work ahead of us:

> With time, and persistence, users (us included) will come to expect PWAs to work. If it's on my home screen, it'll work. The same way as any good native app might work today. (http://bkaprt.com/go/09-06/)

Progressive web apps are driven by three technologies: HTTPS, service workers, and Web App Manifests. Mastering some of those technologies can be tricky, but not insurmountable. The real challenge is figuring out how to apply the technology.

There's no one-size-fits-all service worker. Just as every website offers unique value and must be built with unique constraints, the corresponding service worker script needs to be written to match the site's individual profile.

Service workers give you the opportunity to really make your websites shine. If enough of us rise to the challenge, we can make the whole web shine. Just think—by building progressive web apps, you can make a better World Wide Web. What an opportunity!

I can't wait to see what you build.

ACKNOWLEDGEMENTS

Everyone should experience the joy of working with Katel LeDû and Lisa Maria Martin. From initial discussions right up until the final tweaks, they were unflaggingly fun to collaborate with. Thank you, Katel, for turning my idea into reality. Thank you, Lisa Maria, for turning my initial mush of words into a far more coherent mush of words.

Jake Archibald and Amber Wilson were the best of technical editors. Jake literally wrote the spec on service workers so I knew I could rely on him to let me know whenever I made any factual missteps. Meanwhile Amber kept me on the straight and narrow, pointing out wherever the writing was becoming unclear. Thank you both for being so generous with your time.

Thanks to my fellow Clearlefty Danielle Huntrods for giving me feedback as the book developed.

Finally, I want to express my heartfelt thanks to everyone who has ever taken the time to write about their experiences with service workers. Lyza Gardner, Ire Aderinokun, Una Kravets, Mariko Kosaka, Jason Grigsby, Ethan Marcotte, Mike Riethmuller, and others inspired me with their generosity. Thank you to everyone who's making the web better through such kind acts of openness. To quote the original motto of the World Wide Web project, let's share what we know.

RESOURCES

If this book were a podcast, then this would be the point at which I would be imploring you to rate me on iTunes (or I'd be telling you about a really good mattress). Instead, I'd like to give you some hyperlinks so that you can explore some of the topics in this brief book in more detail.

Explanations

- Mariko Kosaka wrote and illustrated an explanation of service workers in a post on her site called "Service Worker, what are you?" (http://bkaprt.com/go/10-01/).
- Mariko also wrote and illustrated an explanation of promises called "The Promise of a Burger Party" (http://bkaprt.com/go/10-02/).
- Ire Aderinokun wrote a clear guide to "The Service Worker Lifecycle" (http://bkaprt.com/go/10-03/).
- Yoav Weiss has an explanation of different kinds of caching in "A Tale of Four Caches" (http://bkaprt.com/go/10-04/).

Guides

- Lyza Gardner wrote a step-by-step guide for Smashing Magazine on "Making A Service Worker: A Case Study" (http://bkaprt.com/go/10-05/).
- Jake Archibald has collected a series of service worker strategies into an "offline cookbook" (http://bkaprt.com/go/10-06/).
- Jake also recorded an excellent online video series that you can enjoy for free (http://bkaprt.com/go/10-07/).

Examples

- Mike Riethmuller has on offline page on his site that shows articles you've previously visited (http://bkaprt.com/go/10-08/).
- Ethan Marcotte has a similar offline page, but he also shows metadata for each article (http://bkaprt.com/go/10-09/).

- Una Kravets allows you to choose which pages on her site you want to save for reading offline (http://bkaprt.com/go/10-10/).

Progressive web apps

- Alex Russell answers the question "What, Exactly, Makes Something A Progressive Web App?" (http://bkaprt.com/go/10-11/).
- Ada Rose Cannon goes into the details of "The Building Blocks Of Progressive Web Apps" (http://bkaprt.com/go/10-12/).
- Aaron Gustafson quite rightly points out that "Yes, That Web Project Should Be a PWA" (http://bkaprt.com/go/10-13/).
- Jason Grigsby outlines "The Business Case for Progressive Web Apps" (http://bkaprt.com/go/10-14/).

Tools

- Google released a collection of scripts and tools for going offline called Workbox (http://bkaprt.com/go/10-15/).
- To get started with your manifest and service worker, you can paste your website's URL into PWA Builder (http://bkaprt.com/go/10-16/).
- Lighthouse is a great testing tool for progressive web apps that's now bundled into Chrome's Developer Tools under the Audits panel (http://bkaprt.com/go/10-17/).

Documentation

- Over at the website of the World Wide Web Consortium (W3C) you can dig into the details of the Web App Manifest specification (http://bkaprt.com/go/10-18/).
- The ever-evolving service worker specification is on the W3C's Github account (http://bkaprt.com/go/10-19/).

REFERENCES

Shortened URLs are numbered sequentially; the related long URLs are listed below for reference.

Chapter 1

01-01 https://www.w3.org/TR/service-workers/#origin-relativity
01-02 https://certbot.eff.org

Chapter 3

03-01 https://github.com/extensibleweb/manifesto

Chapter 8

08-01 https://madebymike.com.au
08-02 https://ethanmarcotte.com

Chapter 9

09-01 https://fberriman.com/2017/06/26/naming-progressive-web-apps/
09-02 https://w3c.github.io/manifest/
09-03 https://resilientwebdesign.com
09-04 https://thesession.org
09-05 https://archive.dconstruct.org
09-06 https://remysharp.com/2016/05/28/state-of-the-gap

Resources

10-01 https://kosamari.com/notes/Service-Worker-what-are-you
10-02 https://kosamari.com/notes/the-promise-of-a-burger-party
10-03 https://bitsofco.de/the-service-worker-lifecycle/
10-04 https://blog.yoav.ws/tale-of-four-caches/
10-05 https://www.smashingmagazine.com/2016/02/making-a-service-worker/
10-06 https://jakearchibald.com/2014/offline-cookbook/
10-07 https://www.udacity.com/course/offline-web-applications--ud899
10-08 https://madebymike.com.au/writing/service-workers/
10-09 https://ethanmarcotte.com/wrote/going-offline/

10-10   https://una.im/save-offline/

10-11   https://infrequently.org/2016/09/what-exactly-makes-something-a-progressive-web-app/

10-12   https://www.smashingmagazine.com/2016/09/the-building-blocks-of-progressive-web-apps/

10-13   https://alistapart.com/article/yes-that-web-project-should-be-a-pwa

10-14   https://cloudfour.com/thinks/the-business-case-for-progressive-web-apps/

10-15   https://developers.google.com/web/tools/workbox/

10-16   http://preview.pwabuilder.com/generator

10-17   https://developers.google.com/web/tools/lighthouse/

10-18   https://www.w3.org/TR/appmanifest/

10-19   https://w3c.github.io/ServiceWorker/

INDEX

K

Kosaka, Mariko 137
Kravets, Una 138

L

Lighthouse (testing) 138
localhost 8
localStorage 94, 114-117

M

managing space 95
Marcotte, Ethan 118, 121, 137
m-dot 131
method 16
Montulli, Lou 42

N

native apps 133
Netscape 42
networks 1

O

Object-Oriented Programming 14-15
offline first 93

P

patterns 92-93
Pearce, Guy 13
postMessage 97
progressive enhancement 120
progressive web app 120-121
promises 19-24

R

registration 12-18
rejection 21
Resilient Web Design 125
responsive web design 121
Riethmuller, Mike 110, 137
Russell, Alex 138

S

same-origin policy 7
save for offline 110-117, 119
Schwarzenegger, Arnold 13
security 7-8
service worker 3-4
    life cycle 30-32
    updating 32-33
Sharp, Remy 135
strategy
    headers 67
    images 69-74
    pages 69
Sturgeon's Law 134

T

The Session 125
The Washington Post 132
Trivago 65-66

U

URL 4, 133-134
    handling 86-90
    patterns 88-92
user agent 4

V

versioning 54

W

web 1
Web App Manifest 122, 138
web worker 3
Weiss, Yoav 137
Wi-Fi 1
World Wide Web 1
World Wide Web Consortium (W3C)
    123

ABOUT A BOOK APART

We cover the emerging and essential topics in web design and development with style, clarity, and above all, brevity—because we want to help you get back to doing great work.

COLOPHON

The text is set in FF Yoga and its companion, FF Yoga Sans, both by Xavier Dupré. Headlines and cover are set in Titling Gothic by David Berlow.

This book was printed in Germany using FSC certified papers.